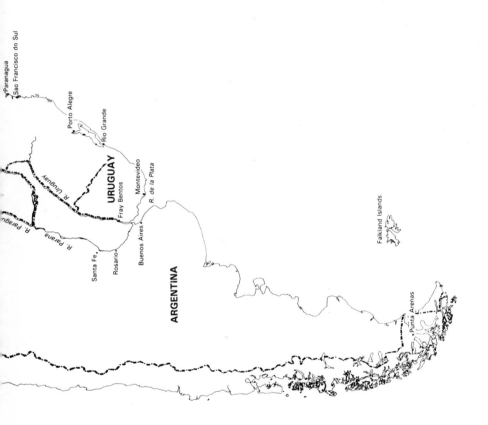

BOOTH LINE

BOOTH LINE

by

P. M. HEATON

THE STARLING PRESS LTD
PRINTERS & PUBLISHERS
RISCA   NEWPORT   GWENT
1987

ISBN 0 9507714 8 1

© First Edition December, 1987: P. M. Heaton

Published by P. M. Heaton, Pontypool, Gwent, NP4 0QF

Printed by the Starling Press Ltd., Risca, Newport, Gwent, NP1 6YB

AUTHOR

Paul Michael Heaton was born at New Inn, Pontypool, in 1944 and was educated at Greenlawn Junior School in New Inn and the Wern Secondary School at Sebastopol. At fifteen he left school and commenced employment, at first in a local store and then with a builders' merchant. A year later he was appointed as a Deck Cadet in the Merchant Navy, with the Lamport and Holt Line of Liverpool, and served in their vessels *Chatham*, *Constable* and *Romney* usually in the Brazil and River Plate trades. He joined the Monmouthshire Constabulary (now Gwent) in 1963 and has served at Abergavenny, Cwmbran, Newport, the Traffic Department and as the Force Public Relations Officer, and now holds the rank of Inspector.

He has always maintained an interest in maritime history, and since 1977 has had numerous articles published in the magazine *Sea Breezes*. He has had the following books published:

Reardon Smith 1905-1980

The Redbrook: A Deep-Sea Tramp

The Usk Ships

The Abbey Line

Reardon Smith Line

The South American Saint Line

Welsh Blockade Runners in the Spanish Civil War

Lamport & Holt

Tatems of Cardiff

The Baron Glanely of St. Fagans and W. J. Tatem Ltd. (with H. S. Appleyard)

Kaye, Son & Co. Ltd. (with K. O'Donoghue)

ACKNOWLEDGEMENTS

In compiling this history of the Booth Line I would like to acknowledge my appreciation for the wealth of information and assistance freely given by the following:—

To the management and staff of the Booth Steamship Co. Ltd.; the World Ship Society Central Record Team, past and present—Messrs. G. H. Somner, H. A. Appleyard, K. O'Donoghue, P. L. White, A. L. Bland, L. Gray and the Rev. D. Ridley Chesterton; Cardiff Central Reference Library, Newport Reference Library; The National Museum of Wales— Welsh Industrial and Maritime Museum, Cardiff; Messrs. W. A. Laxon, E. K. Haviland, R. L. Grayson, P. Thomas, W. Say, A. J. Tennent, D. Burrell, J. Lingwood and Capt. J. S. Garrett.

To the following who have kindly provided photographs—A. Duncan, Gravesend; Newton-Ellis and Company, West Kirby; Tom Rayner, Ryde, Isle of Wight; Skyfotos Ltd., New Romney; and the World Ship Photo Library.

A special thank you goes to Mr. C. J. M. Carter, the former Editor of the magazine *Sea Breezes* for all his help and encouragement throughout the years, and particularly with this project.

CONTENTS

LIST OF ILLUSTRATIONS

23. Built by Scott's of Greenock in 1908, the steamer "Manco" was a unit of the Iquitos Steamship Co. Ltd.

24. The liner "Hilary" (2) was built at Dundee in 1908.

25. The "Hubert" (2) was built in 1910 by Barclay, Curle and Co. Ltd., Glasgow. *(A. Duncan.)*

26. The "Hubert" of 1910.

27. The "Stephen" of 1910. *(Tom Rayner.)*

28. The "Pancras" was built at Hebburn in 1911.

29. The "Pancras" of 1911.

30. The "Aidan" of 1911.

31. The passenger liner "Hildebrand" (2) was built at Greenock in 1911. *(Tom Rayner.)*

32. The "Vincent" was bought and sold in 1913. *(A. Duncan).*

33. The "Alban" (1) of 1914. *(Tom Rayner.)*

34. Built in 1915 the "Oswald" was a war loss two years later.

35. The "Basil" (3) of 1928 remained in the Booth fleet until 1950.

36. The "Boniface" (2) of 1928.

37. The "Benedict" (2) was built in 1930 by Cammell, Laird and Co. Ltd., Birkenhead. *(A. Duncan.)*

38. The most famous of all Booth liners was the "Hilary" (3) built in 1931. *(Tom Rayner.)*

39. The "Hilary" as an Infantry Landing Ship in the Second World War. *(Imperial War Museum.)*

40. A post-war view of the "Hilary" with white hull. *(Tom Rayner.)*

41. The "Clement" (3) of 1934 was sunk in 1939 by the battleship "Admiral Graf Spee".

42. The "Crispin" (2) of 1934 was a war loss in 1941.

43. The passenger liner "Anselm" (3) of 1935 became a troopship in 1940 and was torpedoed and sunk a year later. *(Tom Rayner.)*

44. The second "Dunstan" was ten years old when the Booth Line bought her in 1935.

45. Built by Wm. Pickersgill and Sons Ltd., Sunderland as the "Hubert" in 1946, this ship was renamed "Cuthbert" five years later. *(Tom Rayner.)*

46. The "Jutahay" was bareboat-chartered by the Booth Line from Panama Shipping in 1946.

47. Built in the United States in 1945 the "Dominic" (3) was bought in 1947. She was mainly for the service from New York. *(Skyfotos Ltd.)*

48. The "Dunstan" (3) was built by Wm. Pickersgill and Sons Ltd., Sunderland, in 1948. *(Skyfotos Ltd.)*

49. The "Denis" (2) of 1949. *(Skyfotos Ltd.)*

50. The third "Crispin" was built in 1951 for the service from Liverpool to North Brazil and the Amazon. *(Skyfotos Ltd.)*

51. The passenger liner "Hildebrand" was built in 1951 by Cammell, Laird and Co. Ltd., Birkenhead. She was wrecked off Portugal in 1957. *(Tom Rayner.)*

52. The "Vianna" was bareboat chartered from Panama Shipping Corp. from 1951 to 1955. *(A. Duncan.)*

53. The Norwegian built "Vamos" was bareboat chartered for fourteen years from 1954. *(A. Duncan.)*

54. The liner "Hubert" (4) was built by Cammell Laird, Birkenhead in 1955.

55. The "Veloz" (1) was the first of a number of small ships built for the service from New York to the West Indies, North Brazil and the River Amazon. *(A. Duncan.)*

56. The German built motorship "Venimos" of 1956 was bareboat chartered from Salient Shipping Co. (Bermuda) Ltd. *(A. Duncan.)*

57. The "Venimos" was lengthened in 1964. *(Skyfotos Ltd.)*

58. The "Crispin" of 1956. *(Skyfotos Ltd.)*

59. The "Viajero" was bareboat chartered from Panama Shipping in 1957. *(A. Duncan.)*

60. The "Viajero" after lengthening. *(Skyfotos Ltd.)*

61. The "Clement" (5) was built for the Booth Line in 1959. *(A. Duncan.)*

62. The "Clement" after lengthening. *(Skyfotos Ltd.)*

63. The "Bede" joined the fleet in 1961. *(A. Duncan.)*

64. The passenger liner "Anselm" (4) was acquired in 1961. *(A. Duncan.)*

65. The "Anselm" was the largest ship ever operated by the Booth Line. *(Newton-Ellis & Co.)*

66. The "Veras" was built in 1959 for Lamport and Holt and transferred to Booth in 1962. *(A. Duncan.)*

67. Built in 1952 for Lamport and Holt, the "Bernard" spent two periods trading for the Booth Line. *(A. Duncan.)*

68. The "Cyril" (3). *(Skyfotos Ltd.)*

69. Built in 1953 the "Dominic" (4) joined the fleet in 1967. *(Skyfotos Ltd.)*

70. The "Alban" (2) was acquired in 1976 from Norwegian owners. *(A. Duncan.)*

71. The semi-container ship "Benedict" (4) was built for the Booth Steamship Co. Ltd. in 1979 at Rio de Janeiro. *(Skyfotos Ltd.)*

72. The tug "Mars" (2) was built for service in Portugal.

1. INTRODUCTION

The Booth Line is one of Liverpool's smaller but nonetheless well known Liner shipping companies. They have been involved in the North Brazil and River Amazon trade for over 120 years, and at one time were probably the major industrial body in the Rubber Boom of the Amazon Basin. The origins of the business go back to 1860 when Alfred Booth entered into partnership with an American, and set up offices at New York. Therefore as can be seen the business did not actually start in the United Kingdom. This was not for the purposes of shipowning, which came in 1866 when the American had been replaced in the partnership by Alfred's brother Charles. Offices were quickly opened in Liverpool and the entry into shipowning followed. At that time ships were rather ancilliary to the Booth's main business which was the curing and importation of hides.

My own experience of Booth Line ships dates back to the 1960s when I saw the steamer *Dunstan* at Rotterdam, and had the opportunity of going aboard the newly acquired liner *Anselm* at Liverpool in 1961. Those were the days when the company were still operating two passenger liners on the trade as far as Manaos—a thousand miles up the Amazon. Sadly within a few years the passenger trade was given up but the company has been prepared to build new ships with advanced cargo handling equipment to cope with the vast quantities of lumber and other produce carried.

Until 1977 the Booth Line operated to North Brazil and the Amazon from New York, but that trade has since been abandoned and currently the company operate from Heysham via Dublin, Trinidad and Barbados to North Brazil and the Amazon. Since 1986 the company has operated two Dutch flag motorships of modern design on long term time charter, and at the moment does not actually own any of its own ships. However as trade patterns change in the future I would anticipate the emergence of Booths' as owners again in their own right.

This book is an extension of the history of the Booth Line which appeared in the magazine *Sea Breezes* from January to May, 1979, and actually brings the story up to date. As is my usual practice I have given an account of the founders' origins and early careers, followed by the entry into shipowning and of the various developments in the company's history over the years. I would add that this book concentrates more on the ships and trades of the Booths, and does not deal with their many other interests over the years, including hides, construction and allied businesses.

I hope readers will enjoy this account of the Booth Line's history which has always enjoyed a reputation out of all proportion to its size or the number of ships operated. Many refer to Booths with affection and pride.

P. M. HEATON
December, 1987.

2. ALFRED AND CHARLES BOOTH, THEIR ORIGINS AND EARLY CAREERS.

Alfred Booth who was born in 1834, and Charles born in 1840, were the sons of Charles Booth, a corn merchant in the firm of Thomas Booth and Company, founded at Liverpool towards the end of the 18th century by his father and uncle. The earlier generations, apart from their participation in the corn trade, also had interests in shipping, and indeed Charles Booth senior held shares in a number of sailing ships and early steamers of James Moss and Company, Lamport and Holt and Rathbone Brothers.

The Lamport and Holt Line had been founded in 1845 by Charles Booth senior's cousin, William James Lamport and friend George Holt. Five years later, when it became apparent that the corn business was not going to support a third generation of the Booth family, Alfred at the age of sixteen was apprenticed to Lamport and Holt. Six years later the young Charles Booth followed his brother into the offices of Lamport and Holt, where he too was to receive his early commercial training. It is interesting to note that at this time George Holt's brother Philip, who later married the Booth brothers' elder sister Anna, held a small interest in this rapidly growing company. Another of the Holt brothers, Alfred had spent a short period employed by Lamport and Holt prior to entering shipowning on his own account. Thus all three families, the Booths, Holts and Lamports were united in friendship, through marriage, and in a third way, through religion, as they were all Unitarians.

In 1857 Alfred Booth completed his training with Lamport and Holt, and spent the next three years in the New York offices of Rathbone and Company. With the experience thus gained, in 1860 he entered into partnership with an American, a Mr. Walden, trading as Walden and Booth, with offices in New York, and with the principal objective of importing hides into the United States. These were the days when the connections between Liverpool and New York were greater than those between Liverpool and London. Additional revenue was obtained when Alfred Holt appointed the partners as New York agents for his fleet of steamers which had been trading between Liverpool, the West Indies and New York since 1856. This fleet consisted of the following steamers:—

Name	Year Built	Gross Tons
Cleator	1854	341
Saladin	1856	510
Plantagenet	1859	695
Talisman	1860	738
Askalon	1861	875
Crusader	1862	901

In 1863 Walden retired from the business due to ill health, and Charles joined his brother in the partnership, which was reconstituted as Booth and Company in New York. At the same time with the establishment of offices at 5, India Buildings, Liverpool, Alfred Booth and Company was formed in the United Kingdom.

The partners lost the shipping agency at New York in 1864 when Alfred Holt sold all but one of his fleet of steamers to his main competitor, the West India and Pacific Steamship Company. The older ship, the *Cleator* was retained, and used in the experiments with an engine making more economical use of fuel. At this time Philip Holt left Lamport and Holt and joined his brother Alfred at 1, India Buildings, Liverpool, where they laid the plans for their service to China and the Far East which commenced in April, 1866.

3. THE ENTRY INTO SHIPOWNING

Whilst Alfred and Philip Holt were studying plans for a Far East service, the Booth brothers also explored the possibility of entering shipowning, and with their limited capital resources decided to establish a two ship fleet trading from Liverpool to the North Brazilian ports of Ceara, Maranham and Para (now known as Fortaleza, Sao Luiz and Belem) which hitherto had been served only by sailing ships. It was thought that two steamers would be able to provide sufficient regularity of sailings to make the venture a success.

With the help of Alfred Holt the specification of the two ships was drawn up and an order placed early in 1865 with Hart and Sinnot of Liverpool. First to be launched, later that year was the *Augustine*, a schooner-rigged iron steamer of 1,106 gross tons; she was followed early in 1866 by the brig-rigged steamer *Jerome* of 1,090 gross tons. Both ships had accommodation for twenty-five saloon and fifty steerage passengers. As was common practice in those days, the ships were divided into 64 shares, of which the partners took a fair number, the rest being taken up by relatives and friends including Alfred and Philip Holt, who were also to assist with the maintenance of the Booth ships for a number of years.

The service began on February 15, 1866 when the *Augustine* sailed from Liverpool on her maiden voyage to Para with Charles Booth on board, making calls outward and homeward at Lisbon, Ceara and Maranham. She was followed into service by the *Jerome* three months later and soon after by the *Cleator*, chartered from Alfred Holt and Company for a few voyages.

Thus the Booths quickly became established in the trade, and for three years were to be the only line of steamers so engaged. However the venture did not initially provide very high returns, and when the *Jerome* was involved in a collision for which she was adjudged to blame, the payments that the partners had to make as a result were to further stretch their resources. Therefore in these early years the ships operated largely with the support provided by Rathbone and Company, Lamport and Holt and Alfred Holt and Company.

In 1869 a third ship, the *Ambrose* of 1,168 gross tons was delivered from the yard of A. Leslie and Company, Hebburn on Tyne.

During this year R. Singlehurst and Company of Liverpool, who had been engaged in the North Brazil trade with sailing ships for many years, founded their Red Cross Line and took delivery of three new steamers of 1,300 gross tons, the *Paraense, Maranhense* and *Cearense* from T. Royden and Sons, Liverpool. Thereafter the two companies ran in competition with each other, but by 1870 agreement was reached and the trade was divided between them, providing a fortnightly service. No sooner had agreement been reached than another firm, Hugh Evans and Company, founded their Maranham Steamship Company with two new ships. The following year competition ceased when the newcomer agreed to confine its service basically to a direct Maranham sailing.

During 1870 a fourth ship, the *Bernard* (915 gross tons) joined the Booth fleet from T. Royden and Sons, but during that Spring Singlehursts lost their *Paraense* when she was wrecked at Ceara. This left an imbalance between the two major fleets, and to redress this Singlehursts placed an order for two steamers of 1,600 gross tons with Roydens. These new ships, the *Lisbonense* and *Paraense* (2) were delivered during 1871. With their delivery the number of steamers engaged in the North Brazil trade amounted to ten, Singlehurst and Booth accounting for four each and Evans' two.

At about this time calls at Havre were included in the service, and the Red Cross Line ships alone occasionally extended their voyages to include a call at Manaos, 1,000 miles up the River Amazon. Passengers accounted for an important part of the income of the three lines, steerage passengers from Lisbon with Portuguese emigrants particularly so. Cargo on the outward passages usually comprised consumer goods, and homeward cotton, and later sugar and coffee accounted for an important proportion of total traffic handled. As expected competition, usually of short duration, was encountered in these early decades by the three companies, particularly as regards the Havre calls from French flag tonnage, but this was successfully countered. During this period and subsequently all three were also to be responsible for the carriage of cargo coastwise between the Brazilian ports served.

In 1879 the Red Cross Line added the new *Amazonense* (1,865 gross tons) to their fleet, followed the next year by the *Theresina* (1,145 gross tons), acquired from W. Dodd of Liverpool, and which dated from 1876. At the same time the *Maranhense* after eleven years in the fleet was disposed of and after a succession of owners was finally broken up in 1912.

During 1879 the Booth Line moved its head office in Liverpool to 14, Castle Street. The following year saw the arrival of an additional vessel in the fleet, when the *Mirfield* was acquired from J. B. Crawhall and Company, London. This ship of 1,185 gross tons was built nine years earlier by Scott and Company, Greenock. In 1882 she was renamed *Basil*.

4. THE BOOTH STEAMSHIP CO. LTD.

Having owned ships for fifteen years the partners decided to transfer the ownership of the vessels from the 64 share system to a limited company. Thus the Booth Steamship Co. Ltd. was formed on June 24, 1881. The following was the share position of the four earliest ships in detail prior to the formation of the Booth Steamship Co. Ltd. (*A Liverpool Merchant House* by A. H. John—George Allen and Unwin Ltd., 1959.)

AUGUSTINE

Shareholders	No. of Shares
Alfred Booth and Company	49
Philip Holt	8
Alfred Holt	2
Robert Durning Holt	2
Hester Holt	2
James Quinn	1

JEROME

Shareholders	No. of Shares
Alfred Booth and Company	49
Philip Holt	8
Alfred Holt	2
Robert Durning Holt	2
Hester Holt	2
James Quinn	1

AMBROSE

Shareholders	No. of Shares
Alfred Booth and Company	20
Philip Holt	8
Alfred Holt	2
Robert Durning Holt	2
Hester Holt	2
John Eills	4
William Thornley	2
T. B. Gunston	24

Shareholders	No. of Shares
Alfred Booth and Company	33
Philip Holt	10
Alfred Holt	2
Robert Durning Holt	2
Hester Holt	2
John Eills	4
William Thornley	2
John Philips	1
T. B. Gunston	8

Following the formation of the Booth Steamship Co. Ltd. the majority of these people took shares in the new company. As can be seen, apart from the controlling interest held by the partners in Alfred Booth and Company, the Holt family were the largest other shareholders.

In 1881 a sixth steamer joined the Booth fleet, when the *Barbary* (1,227 gross tons) was acquired from David MacIver and Company. She dated from 1877 when she was completed by Lairds at Birkenhead; after two years under the Booth houseflag she was renamed *Clement*. The Booth Line also acquired a 194 ton wooden barque to carry cargoes of a lower value which did not require the faster passage time of the steamers. This ship, the *Carrie Dingle* had been built in 1873 at Plymouth, and was first owned by W. W. Dingle of Fowey.

On April 16, 1881 the *Amazonense* was wrecked off St. David's Head, while on a voyage from Liverpool to Para, via Havre. Later in the year the Red Cross Line acquired the steamer *Hindostan* built in 1869 as a replacement, renaming her *Amazonense* (2).

From 1882 the passenger trade was centred on Para, and a new steamer, the *Anselm* (1,562 gross tons) with improved accommodation was built for the purpose by A. Leslie and Company, Hebburn, for Booths, and the *Maranhense* (2) (ex *Blodwen*) of 1,480 gross tons, was acquired by Singlehurst. During this same year the Booth Line and Red Cross Line inaugurated a joint service from Manaos to New York via Para. Thus twenty-two years after Alfred Booth had first established himself at New York, the office there started to handle their own ships.

A second sailing ship was added to the Booth fleet in 1882 when they bought the eight year old schooner *Bessie Dodd* of 174 tons. This ship remained in the fleet for three years, and passed through a succession of owners until on February 4, 1906 she was wrecked at St. Shotts, while on passage Cadiz to St. John's in ballast. Her consort the *Carrie Dingle* was sold in 1885 to Singlehursts, and four years later on April 6, 1889 she sank in the English Channel after a collision, while on passage Portmadoc to Hamburg.

During 1883 two ships were added to the Red Cross Line, the *Manauense* (1,672 gross tons) (ex *Bowen*) of 1874, and the *Portuense* (1,470 gross tons) (ex *Abdiel*) of 1875. The following year Booth also added two ships, the *Lanfranc* (1,657 gross tons) and the *Cyril* (1,190 gross tons). The former was built by T. Royden and Sons, Liverpool, while the *Cyril*, two years old, was acquired from other owners for whom she had traded as the *Pacaxo*. During this year the *Sobralense* (1,982 gross tons) was delivered to the order of the Red Cross Line by the Barrow Shipbuilding Company. These three ships were principally for the passenger trade from Liverpool to Para via Lisbon. During the mid-1880s the continental ports of Antwerp and Hamburg were added to the service, and in Portugal calls at Oporto were made in addition to Lisbon.

Three years were to pass before Singlehursts acquired any additional tonnage. In 1887 they took delivery of the *Grangense* of 420 gross tons from the Barrow Shipbuilding Company for service on the Amazon.

In 1887 Alfred Booth retired from the active management of the business and devoted his time and energy thereafter to the arts, literature and education, although he remained a partner until his death in 1914.

It was about that time that both companies started to acquire fleets of tugs and lighters for service at North Brazilian and Amazon ports, for the collection and distribution of cargo to outlying areas, and thereby allowing a more rapid schedule of sailings for the steamers in the trade. A number of old steamers were purchased and hulked in the region for storage purposes.

During 1889 the Booth company acquired the nine year old French steamer *Laurium* (1,498 gross tons) and renamed her *Gregory*. Up until this time, even though they had been shipowners for twenty-three years, the Booth Line had not sold any of their fleet of steamers. However in 1889 the *Bernard* was disposed of to American flag owners, surviving thereafter until October 19, 1897 when she was wrecked at Port Morant, Jamaica, while on passage from Boston.

The following year the *Jerome* was sold, trading thereafter as the *Murcia* until delivered to shipbreakers in January, 1898. In 1890 Singlehursts sold the *Grangense* to Brazilian owners, and there occurred the loss of the *Portuense* which foundered near Angada, 250 miles from the Bahamas on August 28, while on passage Baltimore to Para. During this year two ships were acquired by the Booth Line from other owners, the *Justin* (1,774 gross tons) (ex *Ponca*) and the *Origen* (1,612 gross tons) (ex *Gloamin*).

In 1891 the Red Cross Line took delivery of the *Obidense* (2,380 gross tons) from T. Royden and Sons, Liverpool, and a year later the *Grangense* 2,161 gross tons) which had been completed only a matter of a few months earlier by Palmer and Company, Newcastle, as the *Ruggiero Settimo* for the Italo-Britannica Royal Italian Mail Steam Navigation Co. Ltd. At the same time Booth sold their pioneer steamer, the *Augustine* for further trading, and she survived until March 2, 1906 when she was wrecked off Benghazi while on passage from Tripoli. Her place was taken by the *Hilary* of 1,930 gross tons, which dated from 1889 when completed as the *Red Sea*.

The *Ambrose* was sold in 1893 to J. M. Lennard and Sons,

Middlesbrough, for further trading and without change of name she continued trading until January, 1898 when she was broken up at Garston. At the same time as the sale of the *Ambrose* the first of a two ship order, the *Hildebrand* was delivered from the Aberdeen yard of Hall, Russell and Company. Her sister ship, the *Hubert* was delivered early the following year. Both of these ships of almost 2,000 gross tons, were designed primarily with the direct Para service in mind and consequently they had increased passenger accommodation.

Two ships joined the Red Cross Line during 1894, and they too were for the Para service. Both had been built in 1891 by Palmer and Company, Newcastle, for the Italo-Britannica Royal Italian Mail Steam Navigation Co. Ltd., of London, as the *Principe Di Napoli* and *Carlo Prerio*. Of approximately 2,150 gross tons, they were renamed *Fluminense* and *Cametense* respectively. The following year a further two ships joined the Red Cross fleet, while one was disposed of. The acquisitions were the *Didam* and *Dubbeldam* from the Holland-America Line. Both of 2,800 gross tons, and built four years earlier, they were the largest ships in the Red Cross fleet at the time, and were renamed *Santarense* and *Madeirense* respectively. However, the following year on June 18 the *Santarense* was lost in the North Atlantic following a collision with the barque *Dundonald*, while on passage Liverpool to Para. The ship disposed of was the *Maranhense* which passed to the French flag, and after a succession of owners was finally broken up by T. W. Ward at Inverkeithing in 1925.

Meanwhile, during 1895 the Booth Line had decided to acquire additional ships of increased size in order to carry a proportion of the vast amount of bulk cargoes which were being shipped to the Amazon region in tramp steamers and sailing ships. However it was recognised that the additional ships so engaged by Booth would be unable to find homeward cargo from Brazil, so that they were sent in ballast to Galveston to load cotton for the homeward leg of the voyage. The first two ships acquired for this slower service in 1895 were the *Dominic* of 2,966 gross tons built by Barclay, Curle and Company, Glasgow, and the three year old *Horatio* (ex *Horsley Tower*) from the Wilson Line of Hull. At 3,212 gross tons this ship represented the largest vessel in the fleet up to that date.

The following year saw the arrival of three ships for this trade. The *Dunstan* and *Polycarp*, both of 3,000 gross tons, sister ships of the *Dominic*, which were delivered by Barclay, Curle and Company, and the steamer *Grantully Castle* (3,507 gross tons) dating from 1879 from Donald Currie and Company, which was renamed *Augustine*, the second ship to bear the name in the Booth fleet. At about the same time Singlehursts sold their *Amazonense* (2) to French owners who renamed her *Saint Augustin*, but she was broken up shortly after at Marseilles. In 1897 two more ships were acquired from other owners; the *Warwick Castle* (2,923 gross tons) another acquisition from Donald Currie and Company, which was renamed *Jerome*, and the *Leyden* (3,457 gross tons) from James Beazley of Liverpool, which was renamed *Benedict*. Both were for the slower service with bulk cargoes.

The same year was to mark a number of developments in the Amazon and North Brazil trades. The first was the decision by the Booth Line and a number of influential Brazilian merchants to form a line of ships to trade coastwise under the Brazilian flag. This company, in which the Booth Steamship Co. Ltd. was to hold a 25 per cent interest was the Empreza Navegacao Gran Para, better known as the Empreza Line. Four of the older Booth ships, the *Basil, Cyril, Clement* and *Gregory* were transferred to inaugurate the new company. They were renamed *Salinas, Braganca, Marajo* and *Guajara* respectively; of these the *Salinas* was wrecked at Maranham during 1904, while the three surviving ships passed to the Lloyd Brasiliero in 1907. The *Marajo* was hulked by them in 1912, and the *Braganca* was wrecked off Aracari in December 1925, while the *Guajara* was to survive until broken up in 1930 after a creditable 51 years afloat. However, during 1901 the Booth Line disposed of their interest in this company.

Without doubt the most important development during 1897 was the introduction of a direct service from Liverpool to Iquitos, Peru, 2,000 miles up the mighty Amazon. Singlehurst formed the Red Cross Iquitos Steamship Co. Ltd. and the following year acquired two steamers of just over 1,000 gross tons for the service. They were the *Harmony* built the previous year, from J. and C. Harrison, London, and the *Paris* from F. C. Strick, which had been built earlier that year. They were renamed *Napo* and *Ucayali* respectively, and during 1899 were joined by the *Javary* (ex *Harlech*) also from J. & C. Harrison. The Booth company formed with others the Booth Iquitos Steamship Co. Ltd., and during 1898 acquired the two year old steamer *Huascar* (960 gross tons) from Hernandez and Company, Liverpool, which entered the fleet without change of name. They also took delivery of the new *Bolivar* (1,016 gross tons) from Hall, Russell and Company, Aberdeen.

Two further steamers joined the main Booth fleet in 1898. They were the sisters *Basil* (2) and *Bernard* (2) each of 3,200 gross tons, although both had been built three years earlier by Workman, Clark and Company, Belfast, for different owners. However, three ships were to be disposed of during this year, the *Anselm, Lanfranc* and *Justin*. The *Anselm* traded thereafter until 1908 when she was broken up at New York, the *Lanfranc* survived until she too was scrapped in 1923. However the *Justin* was wrecked on July 28, 1905, near Conquet, while on passage Bilbao to Dunkirk. Singlehursts disposed of two ships during this year, the *Theresina* and *Manauense*. The former ship was to have a long career, but was wrecked at Zuetina in 1925. The *Manauense*, although passing through a number of owners, only survived for a further five years, being wrecked at Muroran in 1903. During the year they did acquire the fifteen year old steamer *Mara* (1,448 gross tons).

In 1899 the Booth Line sold the *Origen* after nine years in the fleet, surviving until November 13, 1915 when she left Philadelphia for Copenhagen and was lost without trace. At the same time Singlehursts sold the *Cearense*, which at thirty years old had been the only survivor of their three pioneer ships. However she was broken up at Palermo in 1902. Also in 1899 came the arrival of the *Gregory* (2,030 gross tons) (ex *Cresswell*) in the Booth fleet, while two ships joined the Red Cross Line. These were the *Maranhense* (3) (ex *Gulf of Lyons*) dating from 1890, and the *Amazonense* (3) built to their own order by D. J. Dunlop and Company, Glasgow, which in the event was to be the last ship built to their order.

In 1900 the Booth Line acquired the steamer *La Plata* (3,445 gross tons) from the Royal Mail Steam Packet Company. This ship built four years earlier at Newcastle by Palmer and Company entered the fleet as the *Clement*. During the year the Red Cross Line added the *West India* of 2,769 gross tons from Frederick Leyland, renaming her *Cearense*. Dating from 1891 she had been built by the Naval Construction and Armament Co. Ltd., of Barrow for the West India and Pacific Steamship Company, subsequently taken over by Frederick Leyland and Co. Ltd.

At this time the Booth Line moved their offices to Oceanic House, 30, James Street, Liverpool, which was also the headquarters of the White Star Line.

Early the following year the Singlehurst company sold the *Mara* to the Empreza Line of Para, who renamed her *Amazonas*. In 1907 she passed to the Lloyd Brazileiro and was eventually broken up in 1930 after completing 47 years afloat.

5. AMALGAMATION

During 1901 the Singlehurst family decided to withdraw from operating their own fleet of ships, and agreement was reached with the Booths for the two companies to be amalgamated under the title of The Booth Steamship Co. (1901) Ltd. The Singlehurst family continued thereafter to hold a substantial interest in the company for a further twenty years. The joint fleet consisted of twenty five ships, and with the amalgamation of the Booth Iquitos Steamship Co. Ltd. and the Red Cross Iquitos Steamship Co. Ltd., under the title of The Iquitos Steamship Co. Ltd., a further five; altogether totalling a gross tonnage of 70,702. The fleet now consisted of the following vessels:—

THE BOOTH STEAMSHIP CO. (1901) LTD.

Name	Year Built	Gross Tons
Hilary	1889	1,930
Hildebrand	1893	1,988
Hubert	1894	1,965
Dominic	1895	2,966
Horatio	1892	3,212
Dunstan	1896	2,994
Polycarp	1896	3,003
Augustine	1879	3,507
Jerome	1877	2,923
Benedict	1894	3,457
Basil	1895	3,223
Bernard	1895	3,280
Gregory	1891	2,030
Clement	1896	3,445
Lisbonese	1871	1,657
Paraense	1871	1,697
Sobralense	1884	1,982
Maranhense	1890	2,767
Fluminense	1891	2,154
Madeirense	1891	2,831
Cametense	1891	2,184
Obidense	1891	2,380
Cearense	1891	2,769
Grangense	1892	2,162
Amazonense	1899	2,828

THE IQUITOS STEAMSHIP CO. LTD.

Huascar	1896	960
Bolivar	1898	1,016
Napo	1897	1,091
Javary	1898	1,249
Ucayali	1898	1,052

The ships from the Red Cross Line had been somewhat older and smaller, and as will be seen the majority of them were disposed of within the following ten years. Shortly afterwards the interests of the Maranham Steamship Co. Ltd., but no ships, were acquired from Hugh Evans and Company. Thus the Booth Line had a monopoly in the trade, and thereafter set about modernising its fleet. The Amazon tug and lighter fleets were also amalgamated, under Booth and Company, later to become Booth and Co. (London) Ltd.

During 1902 the *Hawarden Castle* was acquired from Donald Currie and Company and renamed *Cyril*. Dating from 1883 she had been built by John Elder and Company, Glasgow, and at 4,380 gross tons she was the largest ship in the Booth fleet. At the same time the *Paraense* was disposed of, surviving until broken up in 1926 after a creditable fifty five years afloat.

The following year the *Ambrose* of 4,598 gross tons was delivered to their order by Sir Raylton Dixon and Co. Ltd., Middlesbrough, and with her arrival she introduced a new standard in passenger accommodation, as cargo capacity was sacrificed in favour of passengers. In 1904 two sister ships, the *Justin* and *Boniface* were delivered from Barclay, Curle and Company, Glasgow, followed a year later by the liner *Anselm* of 5,450 gross tons from Workman, Clark and Co. Ltd., Belfast, for the passenger trade from Liverpool to Para and Manaos.

During this period disposals consisted of the *Lisbonense* and *Sobralense* in 1904, and the *Hilary* in 1905. The *Lisbonense* was subsequently lost on August 19, 1929 in the North Atlantic by fire whilst trading as the *Quimstan*. The *Sobralense* passed to owners based at Hong Kong and was mined off Port Arthur on May 12, 1905. The *Hilary* was to have a long career, until as the Japanese *Toryu Maru* she was torpedoed and sunk on May 2, 1945 West of Chemulpo.

On September 5, 1905 the Booth Line incurred their first marine loss in almost forty years as shipowners, when the *Cyril* was sunk following a collision with the new flagship in the River Amazon, below Para.

The following year saw the arrival of the *Cuthbert* of 3,846 gross tons, from the yard of R. & W. Hawthorn, Leslie and Co. Ltd., Hebburn, and during 1907 a sister ship the *Crispin* from Sir Raylton Dixon and Company, Middlesbrough. Two passenger liners were completed in 1907, the *Antony* (6,446 gross tons) from Hawthorn, Leslie and Company, and the *Lanfranc* from the Caledon Shipbuilding and Engineering Co. Ltd., Dundee. Also acquired in this year was the Portuguese steamer *Dona Maria* (2,581 gross tons) which had originally been built in 1887 as the *Port Fairy* by Wigham

Richardson and Company, Newcastle. On arrival in the Booth fleet she was given her original name of *Port Fairy*. At this time the *Gregory* was transferred to the Iquitos Steamship Co. Ltd., and in 1908 was followed by the *Hildebrand* and *Hubert* which were renamed *Huayna* and *Atahualpa* respectively. They were also joined by a new vessel, the *Manco* of 1,988 gross tons from Scott's of Greenock. In this year the smaller *Huascar* was sold, and after passing through numerous owners was lost as the Spanish *Japsis* when she foundered on March 20, 1933 West of Cabo Sardas.

At this time, and at the height of the Amazon rubber boom, considerable competition was encountered from German flag tonnage, but this was eventually successfully countered. In 1908 an additional passenger liner the *Hilary* (2) of 6,329 gross tons was commissioned from the Caledon yard. At the same time the headquarters of the company was moved to Tower Building, Water Street, Liverpool.

Four ships were disposed of from the Booth and Iquitos fleets during 1909 while none were acquired. The former Red Cross Line ship *Fluminense* was sold to Brazilian owners and after a long career under many flags was broken up in Italy in 1928. Her consort, the *Cametense* became the *Tong Hong*, registered at Penang, later passing to the Singapore flag. She was lost in the First World War on July 27, 1917 when she was torpedoed and sunk in the Mediterranean, South West of Cape Sicie. The *Port Fairy* was sold to shipbreakers, but was quickly resold to Ellerman Line for further trading, and renamed *Italian*. She was finally broken up at Preston in 1913. The Iquitos disposal was the *Boliver* which became the *Paulista*, registered at Santos, Brazil. On June 25, 1913 she was wrecked off Paraty, while on passage Santos to Rio de Janeiro.

Four ships, all former units of the Red Cross Line, were sold in 1910. The *Maranhense* passed to J. J. King and Company, and was broken up by them at Garston. The *Grangense* became the *On Temmouz* of Constantinople and survived until March 7, 1915 when she was sunk by the Russian Navy in the Black Sea. The *Madeirense* and *Obidense* both passed to the Norwegian flag, the former being wrecked at the Bahamas in 1912 and the latter wrecked in 1915 on the Shipwash Sand.

During 1910 five ships entered the fleet; the *Vincent* (986 gross tons) for use on the Amazon, from Mackie, Thompson and Company, Glasgow, and the sister ships *Francis* and *Hubert* (2) of 3,900 gross tons from Barclay, Curle and Company. At this time the Booth Line decided to establish a service outwards to the River Plate, with homeward calls at North Brazil and New York, and entered into negotiations for the purchase on the stocks of four ships from Elder Dempster and Company. In the event only one was taken up, the *Christopher* of 4,416 gross tons, built by the Tyne Iron Shipbuilding Company, Newcastle. Orders were placed for three additional vessels with R. & W. Hawthorn, Leslie and Co. Ltd., Hebburn. The first to arrive was the *Stephen* in 1910, followed by the *Denis* and *Pancras* the next year. A fifth ship for this new service, the *Aidan* came from the Tyne Iron Shipbuilding Company, in the same year. Also delivered was the magnificent liner *Hildebrand* (2) of 6,995 gross tons, from Scott's Shipbuilding and Engineering Co. Ltd., Greenock, the largest ship to join the fleet up until that time.

An interesting order was placed at this time with Cammell, Laird and Co. Ltd., Birkenhead, for a 437 ton steamer, the *Ceara* for use on the Amazon. However before delivery she was sold to Brazilian owners. Two other ships for the Amazon river feeder service were delivered, the 220 ton *Acre* and the *Beni* of 469 gross tons from the Lytham Shipbuilding and Engineering Co. Ltd., of Lytham.

Disposals during 1911 were the last former Red Cross Line ships *Cearense* and *Amazonense*, and the *Horatio, Jerome* (2) and *Bernard* (2). Of these all were subsequently wrecked with the exception of the *Jerome* which alone was broken up.

The Iquitos Steamship Co. Ltd. was absorbed into the main Booth fleet in 1911, although the service to Iquitos was changed little by this transaction. The following year saw three further disposals, the *Polycarp, Augustine* and *Vincent*. The *Polycarp* was sold for further trading, and on June 19, 1942 as the Yugoslav *Bosiljka* was torpedoed and sunk off New Orleans. The *Augustine* (2) was broken up at Falmouth, while the two year old *Vincent* hoisted the Mexican flag as the *Libertad* and on August 3, 1916 she foundered off Cuba.

Early in 1913 the steamer *Fort Salisbury* (4,561 gross tons) dating from 1895 was acquired and renamed *Vincent*, but later that year she was resold, and finally broken up fifteen years later. During that year the small *Napo* was disposed of to foreign owners. However, she survived until September 26, 1942 when she was wrecked off Goole after being extensively damaged by air attack.

Two ships arrived during 1914, the 3,172 ton *Michael* from Sir Raylton Dixon and Co. Ltd., Middlesbrough, and the 5,223 ton *Alban* from the Caledon Shipbuilding and Engineering Co. Ltd., Dundee. Disposals accounted for the *Clement* to the Canadian flag, although she was to be lost as a casualty of the First World War. The *Christopher* passed to Elder Dempster and Co. Ltd., eventually being broken up in 1932. The small *Javary* passed to the United States flag and was lost in 1927, whilst the *Ucayali* was to have a long career, until broken up in 1960, after sixty two years afloat.

6. THE FIRST WORLD WAR

At the outbreak of the First World War the fleet consisted of twenty six ships. A further three were built during the period of hostilities to the company's order, and two were sold to the Admiralty. Of the remainder, eight were lost, seven through enemy action and one as the result of a collision.

By the end of 1914 the three passenger liners *Hildebrand, Hilary* and *Ambrose* had been requisitioned by the Admiralty and converted into Armed Merchant Cruisers, forming part of the Cruiser Force "B" of the 10th Cruiser Squadron. At first the squadron was under the command of Rear-Admiral Dudley de Chair, but from 1916 Vice-Admiral Sir Reginald Tupper took over. Engaged in the North Patrol, the squadron was later utilised on convoy escort duties. However, in June 1915 the *Ambrose* was sold to the Admiralty, and was later converted into a submarine depot ship as H.M.S. *Ambrose*. In 1938 she was renamed H.M.S. *Cochrane*, and was eventually broken up in 1946.

In November, 1917 the *Huayna* (ex *Hildebrand* (1)) was sold to the Admiralty for use as a "Q" ship and in 1919 was resold to commercial owners under the Italian flag as the *Manuel Carsi* and on May 19, 1921 foundered off Cabo Torinana. Throughout the period of hostilities the steamer *Manco* was to serve as a Royal Fleet Auxiliary, at first being stationed at Stornoway, but later serving in the Mediterranean.

The first Booth ship to come into contact with the enemy was the steamer *Benedict* on February 28, 1916, when she was attacked by a submarine with gunfire on the surface. However she fought off the attack with her own gun and escaped.

The first ship lost was the liner *Antony* (Capt. H. Forbes) which was torpedoed and sunk by the German submarine *UC48* off the Coningbeg Light Vessel on March 17, 1917, while homeward bound from Para and Lisbon to Liverpool, with the tragic loss of 55 lives.

Twelve days later, on March 29, the *Crispin* (Capt. F. Bell) on passage Newport News to Avonmouth with troops and horses was torpedoed and sunk by the submarine *U57* fourteen miles South of Hook Point, Waterford. Eight lives were lost. The following month on April 17 the *Lanfranc* under the command of Capt. W. E. Pontet which had been converted into a hospital ship, was torpedoed and sunk by *UB40* four hours after leaving Havre for Southampton with wounded soldiers comprising of 234 British and 167 Germans. 34 lives were lost including fifteen Germans, the 570 survivors were rescued by H.M. destroyer *Badger*, H.M. patrol boat *P37*, H.M. destroyer *Jackal* and the French patrol vessel *Roitelet* and taken to Portsmouth.

Six days later on April 23, the *Oswald* (Capt. J. W. Couch) which had been delivered two years earlier by Sir Raylton Dixon and Company, Middlesbrough, was torpedoed and sunk 200 miles South West of Fastnet by the German submarine *U50* while on a voyage from Sabine, Texas to Liverpool, via Pensacola, with a full cargo of sulphur. The Senior Radio Officer was lost.

On May 12 the same year the *Cuthbert* was attacked off South West Ireland by a submarine, but fortunately the torpedo missed and the ship continued her voyage without further mishap. Three days later the *Pancras* was attacked by a submarine in the Mediterranean while under the command of Capt. W. T. Aspinall. The following is an extract from his report:—

> We arrived at Gibraltar on May 14, 1917 at 5 pm and sailed at 6 pm for Genoa. At 5 am on May 15, a thick fog came down and the engines were put slow. The fog lifted a little at 6.50 am, Sabiral Point being abeam, distance about two miles. A German submarine was sighted right ahead about two miles. Engines were put full speed astern. All hands went to stations and the ship was turned stern on to the enemy, going for all she was worth. About 7 am he commenced shelling us, our gunners returning the fire. He fired about 27 shells which burst all around and one right over us. The only damage he did was one man hit on the back of the head, nothing serious, and to shoot away our signal halliards, with the ensign. We fired 14 shots at him without success. He was just getting our range when we got back into the fog and headed for Adra. We then lost sight of the submarine, but he followed us inshore sounding his whistle, another submarine answering on our port side. At 9.40 am we again sighted the submarine on our starboard quarter, trying to get amidships. At 9.43 am we sighted land ahead and two minutes afterwards ran the ship ashore to avoid being torpedoed. The submarine then disappeared.

The *Pancras* was subsequently salved and returned to service. The submarine involved in the attack was *UC54*. At the time the *Pancras* was on a Government charter employed as Expeditionary Force Transport No: *B8120* transporting horses from the United States to Egypt and trooping in the Mediterranean.

On May 25, the Armed Merchant Cruiser H.M.S. *Hilary* under the command of Commander R. H. Bather, RN, was proceeding to the Shetland Islands for bunkers when she was torpedoed and sunk, in the North Sea. It took a total of three torpedoes to sink the vessel. The following month on June 11 the *Dominic* (Capt. F. Scott) bound for Para via Leixoes and Lisbon, was attacked by a submarine off North West Ireland. The following is from the ship's log book:—

> June 11, 1917, 6.40 pm—Observed periscope on starboard beam. Put helm to starboard and got him astern, then commenced firing at him. He lowered his periscope once or twice and then came to the surface and started to fire at us. Later, his shots beginning to fall very close to us, I commenced using smoke apparatus, taking what advantage we could of it.
> 8 pm—Lost sight of submarine. Used distress signals at intervals trying to make him believe we were still firing at him, as our smoke had made a haze.
> 9 pm—Sighted him again a long way off on starboard quarter; got him astern and he chased us again.
> 9.30 pm—Submarine again opened fire, we as well, his shots again dropping very close—some shrapnel falling on after deck and amidships. I again used

smoke and took all the advantage we could.

10.30 pm—Lost sight of submarine, and darkness setting in, I altered course at time so that our funnel smoke should not be a guide for him to follow. Midnight—Course altered to South and on daylight breaking he was not to be seen. I set course West. Very light wind and sea smooth throughout. The crew behaved well and I was ably assisted by officers and engineers, some of whom had been through it before. I am glad to report that no one was hurt but one man, a Russian, who had his hands burnt by sulphur.

A letter was received from the Admiralty evincing their satisfaction at Capt. Scott's handling of the ship. He was also awarded Lloyd's Silver Medal for Meritorious Service and a sum of £50 in recognition of his conduct on this occasion.

Six days later, on June 17, the *Alban* was attacked by a submarine West of Ireland, but escaped when the torpedo missed.

On July 8 the *Cuthbert* (Capt. D. Morris) was attacked by *U80* South West of Ireland, but escaped by using her gun. At the time she had been on passage from New York to Liverpool. The following month on August 23 the *Boniface* (Capt. D. Wynn-Williams) on a requisitioned liner voyage for the government from New York to Glasgow with general cargo, having been parted from a convoy through heavy weather, was torpedoed and sunk by *U53* seven miles from Aran with the loss of one member of the crew. The crew made land at Burbeg in the ship's boats. On the night of November 11, 1917, the *Basil* (Capt. E. Whitehouse) on her way from Southampton to Boulogne with ammunition, unescorted and steaming without lights was run into by the French steamer *Margaux* and foundered before the boats could be got away. Many lives were lost.

On February 27, 1918 the *Benedict* was attacked by a submarine with gunfire in the Irish Sea, but using her own gun escaped. The same year on May 3, the *Pancras* under the command of Capt. D. Peregrine, was in convoy in the Mediterranean, when she was struck by a torpedo, but Capt. Peregrine, finding that his ship was not sinking, requested that the ship be towed and eventually with assistance of tugs arrived at Malta. Capt. Peregrine was awarded the DSC for his efforts. Eight days later on May 11 the *Alban* was attacked in the Irish Sea, but survived, the torpedo missing. On May 23 the *Hubert* (Capt. J. Knight) survived a submarine attack in the Irish Sea when the torpedo missed. On June 13, the *Gregory* survived such an attack in the North Sea, when the torpedo also missed.

During 1918 two new ships of 3,500 gross tons entered the Booth Line fleet, the *Origen* from the Caledon Shipbuilding and Engineering Co. Ltd., Dundee, and the *Polycarp* from Barclay, Curle and Co. Ltd., Glasgow. However, on June 29, the *Origen* (Capt. W. E. Downing) left Falmouth as one of a convoy of nineteen ships bound for North Brazil on her maiden voyage and the following day at 8.35 pm was torpedoed and sunk with the loss of one life.

Next ship to come into contact with the enemy was the *Benedict* on July 22, 1918, and the following is an extract from the report of her master, Capt. J. W. Williams:—

I left Milford Haven on July 19, 1918, in convoy bound for Sierra Leone.

At 6 pm on July 21, received orders from the commodore to proceed to my destination. I therefore left the convoy. At 8.15 am on July 22, in lat. 45.57N, long. 11.54W sighted a submarine one point forward of port beam. Mast and periscope showing above water, distance 400 yards. Weather conditions at the time—strong South West wind, sea rough, speed of ship 6 knots.

I instantly saw that the angle was too small and the chance of ramming was absolutely hopeless. I therefore ordered the helm hard a-port and brought the submarine on the port quarter when I immediately opened fire. The first round went over, and during the interval of 15 seconds in reloading the gun, the submarine went ahead on his engines, by doing so creating such a wave at the base of the periscope that the upper part of his conning tower must have been just awash.

Second round was fired which dropped directly in the centre of the above mentioned wave, and I am firmly convinced that it was a direct hit. Spotting the fall of the first round, I distinctly saw the ricochet of the shell, but in the second round there was none, which further led me to believe that the second round got home. I continued on an Easterly course expecting every moment to be attacked by gun fire. However, as nothing happened, I thought that most likely the submarine would follow me, on the horizon, for a night attack. At 4 pm a heavy squall was forming in the South West.

I then stood North East to give the submarine an impression that I was bound up channel. Immediately the squall closed down, I swung the ship South (twice) and continued on that course. At 7 pm the weather cleared up, being still daylight. Nothing further was seen of the submarine during the night.

The last Booth Line vessel to be attacked during the war was the *Alban* under the command of Capt. A. Alexander on a voyage from Cardiff to Jacksonville, Florida. The submarine involved was *U152*. The following is Capt. Alexander's account of the action:—

At 4.10 pm ship time on September 24, 1918 in lat. 45.22N, long. 29.44W, steering West, weather hazy with wind West, 3 to 4 miles per hour, moderate swell, I was suddenly attacked by gunfire from the port beam. Seeing the flash of the gun, but not the vessel, I immediately ported to bring the enemy astern, at the same time increasing to utmost speed and carrying out a short irregular zig-zag.

After firing four shells from port howitzer we opened fire with our 4.7 gun, firing altogether 17 rounds, the enemy firing approximately 40 rounds, many of which just missed the ship, amongst them being several gas and shrapnel shells, many pieces falling on board without doing any serious damage.

After being engaged one hour and a quarter, we appeared to have run out of range, as the last few shots fired fell short. Soon after, a wireless call purporting to be from a British naval vessel was picked up, but as a similar tone had previously been noted, I concluded the call was not genuine. After dark, I made considerable alteration of course in case of being followed, but nothing further was seen or heard of the enemy.

Great praise is due to Mr. Pym, chief officer, who conducted the firing throughout the engagement, also to the British members of the stokehold ably assisted by the engineers.

During the period of hostilities a large number of loyal men lost their lives while serving aboard the company's vessels, and many decorations and commendations were made, recognising the efforts made by officers and crews during actions with the enemy.

Meanwhile in 1916 Charles Booth had died, but a second generation of the family had been firmly in control of the business for some years. Charles Booth, who was made a member of the Privy Council in 1904, is perhaps better remembered for his work and writings on the poor and for his efforts to highlight the need for old age pensions. A tablet to his memory was unveiled in the crypt of St. Paul's Cathedral in 1920, he being the only shipowner so honoured.

7. THE INTER-WAR YEARS

At the conclusion of hostilities the fleet comprised nineteen ships, and although a number of other vessels had been managed on behalf of the Shipping Controller during the war, at the conclusion all were handed back. No new vessels were added to the fleet, as no replacements for war losses were considered necessary as the immediate post war years were marked with a contraction in the North Brazil and Amazon trades—the rubber boom had ended.

At this time the Booth Line moved its offices to Cunard Building, on Liverpool's waterfront.

In 1919 the *Atahualpa* (ex *Hubert*) was sold for further trading, surviving until November 29, 1927, when she foundered off Cataria, and on November 22, 1920 the *Gregory* was wrecked on Tutoia Bar, while on passage from New York to Manaos. The following year the *Manco* passed to foreign owners as the *Morazan* and survived until on September 8, 1944, when as the Japanese *Ekkai Maru*, she was bombed and sunk by Allied aircraft in Colan Bay, South West of Manila. The passenger liner *Anselm* was sold to Argentine flag owners in 1922 and renamed *Comodoro Rivadavia*. In 1944 she was further renamed *Rio Santa Cruz* and had a long career, being broken up at Rio de Janeiro in 1959 after fifty four years afloat.

The years following the war had seen no great recovery in the North Brazil and Amazon trades, but South Brazil was enjoying a more stable economy and in these circumstances the voyages from New York and other United States East Coast ports were extended as far South as Rio Grande do Sul. This was in direct competition with the Lamport and Holt Line, control of which was no longer with the friends and relatives of the Booth family. In consequence of this, Lamport and Holt ships started to appear in the Amazon, taking a share of this traffic in retaliation.

Against this background no new ships were added to the Booth fleet. Indeed further sales of older vessels continued, and in 1923 marked the departure from the fleet of the sister ships *Dominic* and *Dunstan* for further trading. While the former ship had a long career before being broken up at Grays, Essex in 1952, the *Dunstan* was lost shortly after her sale, following a collision off Gibraltar. During 1924 the *Benedict* and *Michael* were sold for further trading. The former ship was to survive for a further eight years before being broken up in Italy. Surprisingly, the *Michael* was only ten years old when sold, and five years later on February 1, 1929 she was wrecked near Cape Villano, while on passage Dunkirk to Algiers.

The cargo ships sailed outwards from the United Kingdom and Continent to North Brazilian and Amazon ports, and then did one or two voyages between Brazil and New York before returning to the United Kingdom via Brazil. The first class passenger ships operated via Portugal to Para (Belem) and Manaos.

During 1927 the Booth Line acquired its first ship for nine years when they bought the five year old German built steamer *Claus Horn* (ex *Nord Friesland*) (3,396 gross tons) and renamed her *Dominic*. She was always known as the "German" *Dominic*. Although often employed on ocean voyages, a fair amount of her time was spent carrying lumber from the up-Amazon ports to Belem for transhipment into the larger units of the fleet.

At the same time as the *Dominic* entered the fleet, an order was placed with R. & W. Hawthorn, Leslie and Co. Ltd., Hebburn, for two 4,870 gross ton steamers which were duly completed the following year as the *Basil* and *Boniface*. These ships did not have passenger accommodation, as the secondary class passenger/cargo ships were phased out of the fleet in the following few years. Thereafter all passenger traffic was catered for in the first class ships, whose voyages included calls at Oporto, Lisbon, Madeira, Para and Manaos, and became well known for their "Thousand miles up the Amazon" cruises, which were of course part of their normal voyages.

A further cargo ship was delivered in 1930, coming from the yard of Cammell, Laird and Co. Ltd., Birkenhead. Named *Benedict*, she was a sister ship of the *Basil* and *Boniface* delivered two years earlier. With the arrival of this new ship, the *Justin* after twenty six years in the fleet was sold for breaking up.

For the past eight years the only first class passenger ship in the fleet had been the *Hildebrand*, and with the plan to phase out the secondary ships and replace them with cargo ships, started with the delivery of the three "B" class ships, the management decided to order a second first class ship. Consequently an order was placed with Cammell Laird and Co. Ltd., Birkenhead, for a steamer of increased size with accommodation for 80 first class and 250 third class passengers. Launched on April 17, 1931 as the *Hilary* (7,403 gross tons) she was completed four months later. She was the third ship to carry the name in the fleet, and became without doubt the most famous of all Booth liners. The placing of the order for this ship at a local yard during the great depression was greatly appreciated and was also an act of faith in the North Brazilian trade.

However, after the *Hilary* had been in service for a year, the *Hildebrand* was laid-up, and disposed of two years later.

In 1931 the *Cuthbert* and *Francis* were sold. The former ship was broken up in Italy, while the *Francis* passed to the Moller Line, as the *Rosalie Moller*, surviving for a further ten years until she was bombed and sunk at Suez on October 8, 1941. Further disposals were the sister ships *Denis* and *Pancras* during 1932, both passing to Italian shipbreakers. Also disposed of during this year was the *Dominic* to French owners. Two years later the *Hubert*, *Stephen* and *Hildebrand* were all sold for breaking up.

However during 1934 two new 5,051 ton cargo ships, the *Clement* and *Crispin* were delivered by Cammell, Laid and Co. Ltd., the *Clement* having the distinction of being the 1,000th ship built by this yard.

The following year saw the sale of the *Alban* to Italian owners, her place being taken in the fleet by the ten year old *Dunstan* (2) of 5,149 gross tons, which had originally been built as the *Saint Oswald* for Rankin, Gilmour and Company, Liverpool.

This year also marked the arrival of another first class passenger ship to join the *Hilary*. This new ship was the *Anselm* (3) of 5,954 gross tons, from W. Denny and Bros., Dumbarton.

In 1936 the *Aidan* went for breaking up at Savona, and these various transactions, brought about mainly by the contraction in the Amazon/North Brazil trades, had reduced the fleet considerably to that which had entered the First World War just over twenty years earlier. Competition was still being waged with Lamport and Holt, for a share of the South Brazil traffic from New York and other United States East Coast ports. This latter company had just been reborn under a new board of directors following the fall of the "Kylsant Empire", and as far as possible despatched steamers up the Amazon in retaliation.

In 1936 the Booth Line fleet consisted of only nine ships, two of which were first class passenger ships. However the age of the fleet had been reduced considerably, and the company was well placed to compete for traffic. The nine ships were as follows:—

Name	Year Built	Gross Tons
Polycarp	1918	3,577
Basil	1928	4,873
Boniface	1928	4,877
Benedict	1930	4,920
Hilary	1931	7,403
Clement	1934	5,051
Crispin	1934	5,051
Anselm	1935	5,954
Dunstan	1925	5,149

(acquired in 1935)

During the early part of 1939 it was decided to order two motor coasters for use in the Amazon to provide a feeder service, and consequently an order was placed with Henry Robb Ltd., Leith for two such vessels. Both were to have been capable of 10.5 knots, one was to have had a deadweight of 770 tons and the second was to have been slightly smaller. However the advent of the Second World War caused them to be cancelled.

8. THE SECOND WORLD WAR

At the outbreak of the Second World War the fleet consisted of nine ships of which five were lost during the period of hostilities through enemy action. In addition two ships managed on behalf of the Ministry of War Transport were also lost as the result of enemy action.

The first loss incurred by the company was the steamer *Clement* which under the command of Capt. F. C. P. Harris, fell victim to the German pocket battleship *Admiral Graf Spee*, South East of Pernambuco on September 30, 1939. At the time the *Clement* was on a voyage from New York to Bahia (Salvador) and had left Pernambuco the previous day for the final leg of the voyage. The *Clement* managed to despatch a raider report over her wireless, which was eventually relayed to the Admiralty, and marked the opening move in the search which was to culminate in the Battle of the River Plate on December 13, 1939, and the subsequent scuttling of the German ship off Montevideo four days later. Incidentally, not only was the *Clement* the first ship sunk by the *Admiral Graf Spee*, but she was also the first Allied merchant ship of the war to fall casualty to a German surface vessel. The master and chief engineer W. Bryant were taken aboard the German ship and the *Clement* was sunk by gunfire and shortly after these two were transferred to a neutral steamer. The crew had taken to the boats, some being picked up by another vessel, the remainder landing on the Brazilian coast. The only casualty had been the chief officer, E. Jones, who received slight injuries when the raider's seaplane opened fire on the bridge of the *Clement* early in the action.

The second loss through enemy action was the *Polycarp* (Capt. A. Allan) which was torpedoed and sunk by the German submarine *U101* North West of Ushant on June 2, 1940, while homeward bound from Lisbon to Heysham. Fortunately there was no loss of life.

The *Crispin*, sister ship of the *Clement*, had been requisitioned by the Admiralty in August 1940, and as H.M.S. *Crispin* served as an ocean boarding vessel until February 3, 1941, when she was torpedoed and sunk by the submarine *U107* in the North Atlantic. Two months later on April 6, the *Dunstan* under the command of Capt. S. Pollock, was bombed and sunk by German aircraft North West of Cape Wrath. During the action two of the crew were killed and three injured.

Two weeks later on April 20, the steamer *Empire Endurance* (Capt. W. W. Torkington), managed by the Booth Line on behalf of the Ministry of War Transport, was torpedoed and sunk by *U73*, when about 400 miles West of Hebrides. The crew were to suffer great hardships in the ship's boats following the sinking, and one boat was at sea for twenty days before being picked up by the liner *Highland Brigade*. Of this boat's complement of twenty eight men, twenty had died before rescue, and a further three died aboard the rescue ship, including Capt. Torkington. The total casualties from the *Empire Endurance* accounted for sixty lost from the crew of eighty four.

On July 5, 1941 the liner *Anselm* (Capt. A. Elliott), while serving as a troopship, was torpedoed and sunk by the submarine *U96* 300 miles North of the Azores whilst in convoy. Four of her crew were lost together with a large number of service personnel. The final loss suffered by the company was the managed vessel *Fort La Maune* (Capt. J. W. Binns) which was torpedoed and sunk by *U188* in the Indian Ocean on January 25, 1944.

The *Hilary* had an interesting career throughout the war. Initially, she was left on her commercial service with the company, but in January, 1941 she was fitted out as an ocean boarding vessel, serving mostly in home waters. On May 3, 1941 she intercepted the Italian tanker *Recco* about 350 miles North of the Azores, but was unable to stop her crew from scuttling her. However a week later on May 10, she captured the Italian tanker *Ginna M*, which had previously left Las Palmas, and a prize crew took her into Belfast Lough. On April 15, 1942 she was paid off by the Admiralty and returned to commercial service with the Booth Line. On October 8, that same year, she was serving as commodore ship of a convoy bound for New York when she was struck in way of the engine room by a torpedo. Fortunately the torpedo failed to explode and the ship continued her voyage without further incident. In March, 1943, she was requisitioned again, and converted into an infantry landing ship. As such she was sent to the Mediterranean, and on July 10, 1943 took part in the invasion of Sicily as headquarters ship under Rear Admiral Sir Philip Vian. In September of the same year, she took part in the Salerno landing as commodore ship of the Northern Attack Force, under Commodore G. N. Oliver. In December she returned to the United Kingdom, and in June 1944 took part in the Normandy Landings as flagship of Force "J" again under Commodore Oliver. On September 23, Admiral Vian transferred his flag back to her. The *Hilary* was eventually returned to the company in January 1945.

Throughout the war the Booth Line's ships had come under the Government's directions as regards sailings and cargoes, and indeed, the company's ships had not visited the North Brazilian and Amazon ports for some years before sailings were resumed at the end of hostilities.

During the war the company were appointed to manage a number of ships on behalf of the Ministry of War Transport. They are listed hereunder:—

Name	Gross Tons	Year Built and By Whom
Fort La Maune	7,130	1942 Davie Shipbuilding and Repair Co. Ltd., Lauzon.
Fort Nipigon	7,130	1942 Canadian Vickers Ltd., Montreal.
Samyale	7,200	1943 Bethlehem-Fairfield Shipyard Inc., Baltimore.

Name	Gross Tons	Year Built and By Whom
Empire Flame	7,069	1941 Cammell, Laird and Co. Ltd., Birkenhead.
Empire Voice	6,828	1940 Barclay, Cule and Co. Ltd., Glasgow.
Empire Moorhen (ex *West Totant*)	5,628	1919 Columbia River Shipbuilding Corp., Portland.
Empire Chamois (ex *Pacific Redwood*) (ex *Westmount*)	5,684	1918 Ames Shipbuilding and Dry Dock Co., Seattle.

Of these the *Fort La Maune* and *Empire Endurance* became war losses, as previously mentioned. However, it is interesting to note that the latter ship was originally the German *Alster* which had been captured by the Royal Navy off Vestfjord, Norway on April 10, 1940. The *Empire Moorhen* and *Empire Chamois* were First World War, United States-built ships bought by the Ministry of War Transport in 1941. The former ship suffered from continual engine trouble and on June 9, 1944 was sunk as a blockship at Normandy. The *Empire Chamois* and the other surviving ships, with the exception of the *Empire Voice* which was purchased by Booth, were returned to the Ministry after the war.

During the period of hostilities a large number of loyal men had died while serving aboard the company's vessels. The following were decorated or received official commendations in recognition of their efforts:—

Name	Rank	Award
Allan, A	Captain	OBE
Binns, J. W.	Captain	OBE
Costain, G. M.	Chief Engineer	OBE
Cross, W. H.	Chief Officer	MBE
Davies, D. S.	Chief Officer	MBE & Lloyd's Medal
Elliott, A.	Captain	OBE
Evans, L. J.	Chief Steward	Commended
Fairhurst, A. E.	Lamp Trimmer	BEM
Frith, A. S.	Second Officer	MBE
Harris, F. C. P.	Captain	OBE
Harwood, J. W.	Chief Engineer	OBE
Holman, F. R.	Captain	OBE
Johnson, T.	Boatswain	BEM
Johnstone, J. H.	Chief Engineer	Commended
Jones, T. G.	Third Officer	Commended
Phillips, J. E.	Boatswain	Commended

Name	Rank	Award
Richardson, A. S.	Chief Officer	MBE & Lloyd's Silver Medal
Rowan, J.	Storekeeper	Commended
Rucklidge, P. A.	Third Officer	Commended
Saunders, J. E.	First Radio Officer	Commended
Sayers, L. A.*	Chief Officer (Lt. Comdr. RNR)	Order of Red Star (Russian) and mentioned in despatches.
Shaw, H.	Assistant Steward	Commended & Lloyd's War Medal
Stockwell, E. A.	Carpenter	BEM
Thompson, J. E.	Donkeyman	Commended
Twizell, R.	Boatswain	BEM
Whayman, J.*	Chief Officer (Captain RNR)	DSC & Bar and mentioned in despatches.
White, S. N.	Captain	CBE
Williams, T. E.*	Chief Officer (Lt. Cmdr. RNR)	DSC & mentioned in despatches.

* Those marked thus were while serving with the Royal Navy.

9. ACQUISITION BY THE VESTEY GROUP

At the end of the war the Booth Line fleet consisted of only four ships, the *Hilary* of 1931 and the three sister ships *Basil* (1928), *Boniface* (1928) and *Benedict* (1930). The *Empire Voice* was quickly added to the fleet early in 1946 and renamed *Bernard*.

The directors of the holding company—Alfred Booth and Co. Ltd.—having considered the mammoth task of rebuilding the fleet of the Booth Steamship Co. Ltd., came to the decision to sell the shipowning side of their interests. Competition in the trade from New York with the Lamport and Holt Line had creamed off profits before the war, and although discussions between the two companies for a joint service on this route had taken place, the war had intervened before agreement could be reached. Control of the Lamport and Holt Line had prior to the end of the war passed to the Vestey Group, which had among other interests, ships of their Blue Star Line trading to the East Coast of South America, and when this group made an offer for the Booth Steamship Co. Ltd. and their shipping interests on the Amazon, North Brazil, and at New York and Liverpool, it was accepted. Thus early in 1946 control of the Booth Line passed to the Vestey Group. The company, as with Lamport and Holt, retained their own offices, personnel—shore based and sea going—and their respective fleets of ships.

It was obvious that a fleet of five ships would not be sufficient to maintain both the services from the United Kingdom and New York, and while pre-war the service to and from the United States was maintained by ships fitting in one or two coastwise passages before returning to the United Kingdom, it was now decided to maintain the New York sailings with ships permanently stationed on the coast. Indeed Lamport and Holt had been doing this in the inter-war years.

During 1946, as a first step towards this, two modern motorships of 3,800 gross tons were bareboat chartered from the Panama Shipping Corp. These ships, both built in the United States during 1945, were named *Pachitea* (ex *Coastal Challenger*, ex *Tulare*) and *Jutahy* (ex *Roband Hitch*, ex *Frank J. Petrarca*) respectively. A pre-war imbalance of cargo, whereby homeward bound ships were usually fully laden as opposed to the outward bound vessels having space, which enabled capacity for the carriage of extra coal bunkers, had ensured that while other companies had turned to motorships or oil-fired steamers, the Booth Line fleet had remained coal-fired. The arrival of these two bareboat chartered motorships marked the arrival of the first such vessels in the fleet.

At the same time a contract for a 4,115 gross ton steamer ordered by the Ministry of War Transport from Wm. Pickersgill and Sons Ltd., Sunderland, was taken over, and was duly completed as the *Hubert* (3) for service from the United Kingdom. The size of cargo steamers engaged in the Amazon trade had been dictated by their ability to call at small wharves to collect or discharge cargo. In contrast the first class passenger

41

ships, albeit at this time only represented by the refurbished *Hilary* (now with accommodation for 93 first class and 138 tourist class passengers) only called at Belem (formerly Para) and Manaos, and were therefore not quite so restricted as to size. While it had been expedient to buy the *Bernard* in 1946, by the following year, as more modern and more suitably-sized tonnage arrived, she was transferred to the associated Lamport and Holt Line, marking the first of many such transfers thereafter between the two companies. In 1947 the two year old motorship *Dominic* (ex *Hickory Glen*) of 3,860 gross tons joined the fleet mainly for service from New York.

While hitherto the funnel colours of Booth Line steamers had been plain black, at about this time the houseflag, (white with red cross with blue letter "B" thereon) was painted either side.

Orders were placed with Wm. Pickersgill & Sons Ltd., Sunderland, for two new steamers of almost 3,000 gross tons to replace the older units maintaining the cargo services from Liverpool to the Amazon and North Brazil. The first to arrive was the *Dunstan* in 1948, followed a year later by the *Denis*. With their arrival the older vessels were disposed of, the *Benedict* being transferred to Lamport and Holt in 1948, followed a year later by the *Boniface*. In 1950 the *Basil* was sold to Panamanian flag owners, and a year later was wrecked.

During 1951 the *Hilary* was joined by a second first-class passenger ship, the turbine steamer *Hildebrand* from the yard of Cammell, Laird and Co. Ltd., Birkenhead. At 7,735 gross tons she was a little larger than the *Hilary* but with a far more modern appearance. The arrival of the new ship enabled the Booth Line to cater for the immediate post-war boom in sea travel, and both ships were well known for their Amazon cruises, providing excellent accommodation.

During this year a further ship, the eight year old steamer *Vianna* (2,825 gross tons) was bareboat chartered to supplement the New York service. A new arrival for the Liverpool service was the steamer *Crispin* (4,472 gross tons) from Wm. Pickersgill. At the same time the three year old *Dunstan* (3) was transferred to Lamport and Holt, for service from New York as the *Sallust*. At this time it was decided to reserve the "H" initial for the passenger steamers, and in consequence the *Hubert* was renamed *Cuthbert*.

During 1953 the Vestey Group established a new service based in Singapore, and formed a new company, Austasia Line Ltd. In order to inaugurate the new service a 4,300 ton steamer on order for Booth's at Wm. Pickersgill and Sons Ltd., Sunderland, which it had been intended to name *Clement* was transferred. She was launched as the *Malay Star* and finally completed as the *Malay*. Eleven years later she was renamed *Mahsuri* by the Austasia Line. In addition, the *Cuthbert* (2) and *Crispin* (3) were transferred becoming the *Mandama* and *Mandowi* respectively.

During 1954 the previously chartered *Pachitea* was bought and renamed *Dunstan*, the fourth ship to bear the name in the Booth fleet. At the same time the *Jutahay* was returned to her owners. An additional vessel was bareboat chartered from Panama Shipping in this year. This ship, the 1,090 gross ton *Vamos* had been completed for Norwegian owners two years earlier. She was for service from New York to North Brazil and the

Amazon, and later saw service on a new route from Montreal to the West Indies and British Guiana.

For a short period during 1954 the Booth Line managed the cattle carrier *Drover* operating between Ireland and Liverpool, on behalf of the associated Union Cold Storage Co. Ltd., but this ship was soon sold to other owners.

The following year, 1955, saw the arrival of a new passenger liner, the turbine steamer *Hubert* (8,062 gross tons) from Cammell, Laird and Co. Ltd., Birkenhead. She was a sister ship of the *Hildebrand* and with the older *Hilary* brought the passenger fleet up to three ships. This new ship had accommodation for 74 first and 96 tourist class passengers. During 1956 the service from Liverpool was extended to include calls at Trinidad and Barbados. At about this time the *Hilary* was again refurbished and at the same time her hull colour was changed to white, while other units of the fleet remained black. On returning to service she was chartered to Elder Dempster Lines for a few voyages to West Africa. Thereafter she took her place on the North Brazil service with her two more modern consorts.

However, on September 25, 1957 the *Hildebrand*, on a voyage from Liverpool to the Amazon via Lisbon, went ashore in thick fog near Cascais, while inward bound to the Portuguese port. The passengers were taken off, and after lengthy efforts to refloat the ship, salvage was finally abandoned a month later.

The service by the *Vamos* from New York had proved the viability of ships of about 1,000 gross tons in this trade, particularly in the ability to reach the Peruvian port of Iquitos, and to serve outlying Amazon ports. As a result over the next few years a number of similar ships were acquired, either directly by the Booth Line or on bareboat charter from the Lamport and Holt Line, Panama Shipping Corporation, or the Salient Shipping Co. (Bermuda) Ltd. They included the following vessels:—

Name	Year Built	Builder
Veloz	1955	Norderwerft Koser and Meyer, Hamburg.
Venimos	1956	Norderwerft Koser and Meyer, Hamburg.
Viajero	1957	Norderwerft Koser and Meyer, Hamburg.
Valiente (acquired in 1961)	1959	Norderwerft Koser and Meyer, Hamburg.
Vigilante (acquired in 1958)	1955	Schiffsw. A. Paul, Hamburg.
Veras (acquired in 1962)	1959	George Brown Ltd., Greenock.

43

Name	Year Built	Builder
Crispin	1956	T. van Duivendijk Scheepswerf N.V., Lekkerkerk.
Clement	1959	T. van Duivendijk Scheepswerf N.V., Lekkerkerk.

These ships took over all the New York/Montreal to North Brazil and West Indies sailings, and the remaining cargo vessels, albeit somewhat larger, maintained the service from the United Kingdom.

In 1958 the *Dunstan* (4) after four years in the fleet was transferred to Lamport and Holt as the *Sallust*. At the same time the *Sallust* which had previously been Booth's third *Dunstan* was transferred back to Booth's for service from Liverpool.

On September 15, 1959 the *Hilary* was delivered to Thos. W. Ward at Inverkeithing for breaking up, thus leaving the passenger service to the *Hubert* alone. Two 3,000 ton motorships were transferred to the Booth Line from Blue Star in the period 1960/61. Both were formerly refrigerated ships completed just before the Second World War by Burmeister and Wain, Copenhagen, and had been acquired by the Vestey Group some six years earlier. In the Booth fleet they became the *Basil* (4) and *Bede* and were used to maintain the cargo service from Liverpool.

10. FURTHER DEVELOPMENTS

The *Hubert* had been maintaining the passenger service alone for almost two years, when in the Spring of 1961 the opportunity was taken to acquire a second ship for the service. The Belgian *Thysville* (ex *Baudouinville*) dating from 1950, had previously traded between Antwerp and the Belgian Congo, but with the independence of the Congo, this ship, and indeed her consorts, were put on the sale market. She joined the Booth Line as the *Anselm*, fourth ship to bear the name in the fleet. She was equipped to carry 135 first class and 101 tourist class passengers, and at 10,854 gross tons was the largest ship ever to be owned and operated by the Booth Line. Her size has never yet been exceeded in the fleet.

At the same time the *Dominic* was sold to foreign buyers. Thus in 1962 the fleet comprised the following vessels:—

Name	Year Built	Gross Tons
Anselm (4)	1950	10,854
Basil (4)	1939	3,022
Bede	1938	3,111
Clement (5)	1959	1,565
Crispin (4)	1956	1,593
Denis (2)	1949	2,990
Dunstan (3)	1948	2,993
Hubert (4)	1955	8,062
Valiente	1959	1,312
Vamos	1952	1,090
Veloz (1)	1955	1,312
Venimos	1956	1,309
Veras	1959	1,282
Viajero	1957	1,204
Vigilante	1955	915

Of the fifteen ships, six were employed from Liverpool, the *Anselm* and *Hubert* maintaining the passenger service, while the *Basil, Bede, Denis* and *Dunstan* maintained a cargo only service. The "C" and "V" class ships maintained the New York to West Indies, North Brazil and Amazon service, and the Montreal to West Indies and British Guiana service.

The *Bede* was sold in 1963 to foreign buyers, her place being taken by the *Rossetti* from Lamport and Holt. This ship had been completed in 1956 by Wm. Pickersgill and Sons, Sunderland, and became the *Boniface* in the Booth fleet.

In the early 1960s the agency business, tug and lighter fleets operating at North Brazil and throughout the Amazon under Booth (Brasil) Ltd., were disposed of to Brazilian interests.

The demand for passenger accommodation had been steadily falling, primarily due to the airlines taking most of the traffic, so that in 1963 the *Anselm* was found to be surplus to requirements, and was transferred to the Blue Star Line, becoming the *Iberia Star* for service from London to Brazil and the River Plate. In 1965 she passed to the Austasia Line as the *Australasia* and was finally broken up in Taiwan in 1973. Finally in 1964 the Booth Line withdrew altogether from the passenger trade, and in consequence the *Hubert* was transferred to the Austasia Line as the *Malaysia*. In the same year the *Basil* was also disposed of, passing to Greek interests.

In 1965 another vessel from Lamport and Holt joined the fleet when the *Rubens* (ex *Siddons*) of 4,459 gross tons, which dated from 1952 and was a product of Wm. Pickersgill and Sons Ltd., was transferred to become the *Bernard* (4). During the following year the *Dunstan* of 1948 was renamed *Basil*, and two other ships joined the fleet from the Austasia Line. They were the steamers *Mandowi* (ex *Crispin*) and *Mahsuri* (ex *Malay*) which became the *Dunstan* and *Benedict* respectively, for service from Liverpool. However both were quickly transferred with other vessels to the Lamport and Holt Line, the *Dunstan* later in that year to become the *Rubens*, and in 1967 the *Benedict*, *Boniface* and *Bernard* to be renamed *Renoir*, *Rossetti* and *Rossini* respectively.

In 1967 Lamport and Holt tonnage was withdrawn from New York, and their last two ships on this service, the *Sheridan* of 1961 and the *Spenser* of 1962 transferred to Booth, as the *Cyril* and *Cuthbert*. They were sister ships of the *Clement* and *Crispin*.

Also acquired during 1967 was the 3,324 ton motorship *Makati* from the Austasia Line. This ship, built in 1953 at Aalborg, was originally the Danish *Jonna Dan* and in the Booth Line became the *Dominic*. However, she was quickly sent for lengthening, thus increasing her tonnage to 4,585. She was initially employed from Liverpool, but later spent most of her time trading from New York. It should also be mentioned that most of the smaller motorships trading from New York to the Amazon and North Brazil, were lengthened in the mid-1960s, thus increasing their gross tonnages by approximately 200-300 tons.

During 1967 the twelve year old *Veloz* (1) was sold to owners based at Callao, as the *Atahualpa*. During the late 1960s a slight contraction in the trades to North Brazil was experienced, with the result that in 1968 four ships were disposed of while none were acquired. These were the sister ships *Basil* (ex *Dunstan*) and *Denis*, which had operated from Liverpool, and the small *Vamos* and *Vigilante* which had operated from New York. The following year the *Valiente* was renamed *Veloz*, second ship to bear the name in the fleet. During 1970 two ships which had previously served in the Booth fleet were transferred back from Lamport and Holt, reverting to their former names of *Boniface* and *Bernard*.

A period of quiet stability was experienced during the early 1970s, but the Booth Line were trading as "third flag operators" or "cross traders" from New York to North Brazil, and with the growth of a number of Brazilian shipping concerns and the restrictive legislation concerning cross traders serving the United States, the amount of cargo available for shipment in Booth Line ships fell, and in consequence in 1973 the four remaining "V" class ships—*Venimos, Veloz* (2), *Viajero* and *Veras* were withdrawn from service and sold.

Also disposed of was the *Bernard* to foreign owners, although as the *Berwell Adventure* she was time-chartered back for a short period. The following year the *Crispin* and *Boniface* were disposed of, thus the Booth fleet was reduced to four ships, all of which were trading from New York to the Amazon, North Brazil and the West Indies, i.e. the *Dominic, Clement, Cyril* and *Cuthbert*. Meanwhile the Liverpool sailings were maintained by the time-chartering in the Spring of 1974 of two ships, the Singapore flag *Dollart* and the German *Bilstein*, which were renamed for the duration of the charters as *Ambrose* and *Antony* respectively.

During 1974 the Vestey Group acquired premises at 30, James Street, Liverpool, from the Pacific Steam Navigation Company. This building was erected in 1892 as Oceanic House and was originally the headquarters of the White Star Line, and for a period had also been the home of the Booth Line. The building was refurbished and renamed Albion House. This coincided with the formation of a new company, under the title Blue Star Ship Management Ltd., which took over responsibility for the ship husbandry of all the ships owned and/or operated by the Booth Steamship Co. Ltd., the Lamport and Holt Line Ltd., and Blue Star Line Ltd., and was originally based at Liverpool, but almost a decade later was to be moved to Albion House, Leadenhall Street, London. During the early part of 1975 the managements of both the Booth Line and Lamport and Holt moved to the new building at Albion House, Liverpool.

In 1975 the *Dominic* was sold, further reducing the New York based fleet, which now consisted of the three "C" class ships. In the Spring of 1976 the Booth Line acquired the motorship *Lyra* (4,547 gross tons) from Norwegian owners. Dating from 1971 she had been completed by Schiffswerft Neptun, Rostock. In the Booth fleet she became the *Alban* for service from Liverpool via Trinidad and Barbados to North Brazil and the Amazon. With the arrival of the *Alban*, the chartered *Ambrose*, having completed twelve round voyages, was returned to her owners.

The ten year old steamer "Justin" was acquired by Alfred Booth and Company in 1890.

The first "Origen" was acquired from other owners in 1890.

(World Ship Photo Library)

The steamer "Obidense" was built in 1891 by T. Royden and Sons, Liverpool for R. Singlehurst and Company's Red Cross Line. She passed to the Booth fleet in 1901.

The three year old "Hilary" joined the Booth Line fleet in 1892.

(World Ship Photo Library)

Built for the Booth Steamship Co. Ltd., in 1893 the "Hildebrand" (1) was transferred to the Iquitos Steamship Co. Ltd., in 1908 as the "Huayna".

(World Ship Photo Library)

The "Hubert" (1) of 1894 was transferred to the Iquitos Steamship Co. Ltd., in 1908 and renamed "Atahualpa"
(World Ship Photo Library)

"FLUMINENSE" 1891.

The Red Cross Line acquired the "Fluminense" in 1894. She passed to Booths seven years later.

The "Madeirense" joined the Red Cross Line fleet in 1895.

The "Dominic" was built in 1895 by Barclay, Curle and Company, Glasgow.

(World Ship Photo Library)

The "Dominic" (1) of 1895.

The Booth Line acquired the ''Horatio'' in 1895.

The "Dunstan" (1) of 1896.

BOOTH S.S. CO., LTD.

S.S. JEROME.

(World Ship Photo Library)

Built in 1877 the "Jerome" (2) was twenty years old when acquired by Booths.

The "Basil" (2) joined the fleet in 1898.

(World Ship Photo Library)

Built in 1896 the "Clement" (2) was bought from Royal Mail in 1900.

(A. Duncan)

Built in 1883 the "Cyril" (2) was acquired in 1902.

The passenger liner "Ambrose" was built for the Booth Line in 1903 by Sir Raylton Dixon and Co. Ltd., Middlesbrough.

Built in 1904 by Barclay, Curle and Co. Ltd., Glasgow, the second "Justin" remained in the fleet for over twenty years.

The "Anselm" (2) of 1905 was a product of Workman, Clark and Co., Belfast.

(World Ship Photo Library)

The ''Crispin'' (1) of 1907.

The liner "Antony" (1) was built in 1907 by R. & W. Hawthorn, Leslie and Co. Ltd., Hebburn.

The passenger liner "Lanfranc" of 1907.

(Tom Rayner)

Built by Scott's of Greenock in 1908, the steamer "Manco" was a unit of the Iquitos Steamship Co. Ltd.

The liner "Hilary" (2) was built at Dundee in 1908.

The "Hubert" (2) was built in 1910 by Barclay, Curle and Co. Ltd., Glasgow.

(A. Duncan)

The "Hubert" of 1910.

The "Stephen" of 1910.

(Tom Rayner)

The "Pancras" was built at Hebburn in 1911.

The "Pancras" of 1911.

The "Aidan" of 1911.

The passenger liner ''Hildebrand'' (2) was built at Greenock in 1911.

(Tom Rayner)

The "Vincent" was bought and sold in 1913.

(A. Duncan)

The "Alban" (1) of 1914.

(Tom Rayner)

Built in 1915 the "Oswald" was a war loss two years later.

The "Basil" (3) of 1928 remained in the Booth fleet until 1950.

The "Boniface" (2) of 1928.

The "Benedict" (2) was built in 1930 by Cammell, Laird and Co. Ltd., Birkenhead.   (A. Duncan)

The most famous of all Booth liners was the "Hilary" (3) built in 1931.

(Tom Rayner)

The "Hilary" as an Infantry Landing Ship in the Second World War.

(Imperial War Museum)

A post-war view of the "Hilary" with white hull.

(Tom Rayner)

The "Clement" (3) of 1934 was sunk in 1939 by the battleship "Admiral Graf Spee".

The "Crispin" (2) of 1934 was a war loss in 1941.

The passenger liner "Anselm" (3) of 1935 became a troopship in 1940 and was torpedoed and sunk a year later. (Tom Rayner)

S.S. "DUNSTAN" (1925)
Ex ADBORDES '35

The second "Dunstan" was ten years old when the Booth Line bought her in 1935.

Built by Wm. Pickersgill and Sons Ltd., Sunderland as the "Hubert" in 1946, this ship was renamed "Cuthbert" five years later.
(Tom Rayner)

The "Jutahay" was bareboat-chartered by the Booth Line from Panama Shipping in 1946.

Built in the United States in 1945 the "Dominic" (3) was bought in 1947. She was mainly for the service from New York.
(Skyfotos Ltd.)

The "Dunstan" (3) was built by Wm. Pickersgill and Sons Ltd., Sunderland, in 1948.

(Skyfotos Ltd.)

The ''Denis'' (2) of 1949.

(Skyfotos Ltd.)

The third "Crispin" was built in 1951 for the service from Liverpool to North Brazil and the Amazon. (Skyfotos Ltd.)

The passenger liner "Hildebrand" was built in 1951 by Cammell, Laird and Co. Ltd., Birkenhead. She was wrecked off Portugal in 1957.

(Tom Rayner)

The "Vianna" was bareboat-chartered from Panama Shipping Corp. from 1951 to 1955.

(A. Duncan)

The Norwegian built "Vamos" was bareboat-chartered for fourteen years from 1954.

(A. Duncan)

The liner "Hubert" (4) was built by Cammell Laird, Birkenhead in 1955.

The 'Veloz'' (1) was the first of a number of small ships built for the service from New York to the West Indies, North Brazil and the River Amazon.

(A. Duncan)

The German built motorship "Venimos" of 1956 was bareboat-chartered from Salient Shipping Co. (Bermuda) Ltd.

(A. Duncan)

The "Venimos" was lenghthened in 1964.

(Skyfotos Ltd.)

The "Crispin" of 1956.

The "Viajero" was bareboat-chartered from Panama Shipping in 1957.

(A. Duncan)

The "Viajero" after lengthening.

(Skyfotos Ltd.)

(A. Duncan)

The "Clement" (5) was built for the Booth Line in 1959.

(Skyfotos Ltd.)

The "Clement" after lengthening.

The "Bede" joined the fleet in 1961.

(A. Duncan)

The passenger liner "Anselm" (4) was acquired in 1961.

(A.Duncan)

The "Anselm" was the largest ship ever operated by the Booth Line.

(Newton-Ellis & Co.)

The "Veras" was built in 1959 for Lamport and Holt and transferred to Booth in 1962.

(A. Duncan)

Built in 1952 for Lamport and Holt, the "Bernard" spent two periods trading for the Booth Line.

(A. Duncan)

The "Cyril" (3)

(Skyfotos Ltd.)

Built in 1953 the "Dominic" (4) joined the fleet in 1967.

(Skyfotos Ltd.)

The "Alban" (2) was acquired in 1976 from Norwegian owners.

(A. Duncan)

The semi-container ship "Benedict" (4) was built for the Booth Steamship Co. Ltd., in 1979 at Rio de Janeiro. (Skyfotos Ltd.)

The tug "Mars" (2) was built for service in Portugal.

11. CONTAINERISATION

At the end of 1975 Mr. Edmund Vestey, chairman of the Booth Steamship Co. Ltd., signed a contract with the Brazilian shipyard of EMAQ—Engenharia e Maquinas S.A., Rio de Janeiro, for the construction of four semi-container motorships, each of 3,636 gross tons, capable of 15 knots, and with a bale capacity of 323,000 cu. ft. and of carrying 133 containers, 33 of them on deck. Two were for service from Liverpool and two from New York.

The chartered *Antony* was returned to her owners in April 1977, and her place was taken by the time-chartering of other vessels, including the Liverpool registered *Helen Miller* for a period, to supplement the *Alban*. With the impending arrival of the new ships, the *Alban* was sold late in 1978 to the Chinese.

During the Spring of 1977, the amount of cargo available for shipment between New York and North Brazil had fallen considerably, and indeed the service was running at a loss, which could no longer be tolerated indefinitely. Consequently the service was abandoned, and the three ships, *Cuthbert, Cyril* and *Clement* were brought back to Liverpool and subsequently sold.

With the withdrawal from New York, the order at the Brazilian shipyard was reduced to two ships, for the Liverpool service. The first was launched on August 4, 1978 as the *Benedict* (4) and was followed by the launching of the *Boniface* (4) on October 31. They entered service during 1979 and proved highly successful, being particularly useful vessels which apart from their container capacity were also able to lift the large quantities of hard wood exported from the Amazon region.

However, there has been a dramatic change in British shipping during the last decade, which has resulted in the loss to the British flag of a considerable number of vessels. One aspect of this has seen the situation whereby an operator can charter in tonnage far cheaper than he can operate his own ships. As a result in 1986 the relatively new *Benedict* and *Boniface* were disposed of to Yugoslavian owners, and their place on the trade from the United Kingdom, where the port of Heysham is now used, to North Brazil and the Amazon, via Dublin, Trinidad and Barbados, has been taken by the chartering in of two Dutch flag motorships of 3,986 gross tons (6,025 tons deadweight) which were built in 1985. They have been renamed for the duration of the charters as the *Clement* and *Crispin*.

Thus at present the Booth Line whilst still operating in their traditional trade to the Amazon and North Brazil are without any of their own ships. This situation will no doubt be remedied in due time, and will hopefully reflect an upturn in the fortunes of British Shipowners.

APPENDICES

12. APPENDIX ONE
BOOTH LINE—FLEET LIST

Name and Period in Fleet	Gross Tons	History
Augustine (1) 1865-1892	1,106	1865 built by Hart and Sinnot, Liverpool, for Booth; 1892 to F. Pace, Malta; 2.3.1906 wrecked Benghazi while on passage from Tripoli.
Jerome (1) 1866-1890	1,090	1866 built by Hart and Sinnot, Liverpool, for Booth; 1890 to Goodyear and Company, Liverpool, renamed Murcia; 1.1898 to J. J. King, Garston for breaking up.
Ambrose (1) 1869-1893	1,168	1869 built by A. Leslie and Company, Hebburn, for Booth; 1893 to J. M. Lennard and Sons, Middlesbrough; 10.1897 to J. J. King, Garston, intended for breaking up, but resold to Cory Bros., and converted for use as a coal hulk on the Thames.
Bernard (1) 1870-1889	915	1870 built by T. Royden and Sons, Liverpool, for Booth; 1889 to Baltimore Fruit Company, U.S.A.; 1893 to Boston Fruit Company, U.S.A.; 19.10.1897 wrecked at Port Morant, Jamaica, while on passage from Boston.
Mirfield Basil (1) 1880-1897	1,185	1871 built by Scott and Company, Greenock, as Mirfield for J. B. Crawhall and Company, London; 1880 to Booth; 1882 renamed Basil; 1897 to Empreza Navegacao Gram Para (F. Gomes and Company) Para, renamed Salinas; 10.1904 wrecked at Maranham.
Barbary Clement (1) 1881-1897	1,227	1877 built by J. Laird, Birkenhead, as Barbary for D. MacIver and Company, Liverpool; 1881 to Booth; 1883 renamed Clement; 1897 to Empreza Navegacao Gram Para (F. Gomes and Company), Para, renamed Marajo; c1900 to Cia de Cabotagem do Gras Para, Para; 1907 to Lloyd Brasileiro; 1912 converted to a hulk.
Carrie Dingle 1881-1885	194	Wooden barque. 1873 built by Williams, Plymouth, as Carrie Dingle for W. W. Dingle, Fowey; 1881 to Booth; 1885 to Singlehurst; 6.4.1889 sank in the English Channel after a collision, while on passage Portmadoc to Hamburg.

Name and Period in Fleet	Gross Tons	History

Bessie Dodd
1882-1885
174
Wooden schooner. 1874 built by Westcott, Barnstaple, as *Bessie Dodd* for Preston Shipowners Co. Ltd., Preston; 1882 to Booth; 1885 to W. Jago; Liverpool; 1890 to W. Pearce, Liverpool; 1893 to J. H. Nicholls, Falmouth; 1897 to A. Nicholls, Falmouth; 1904 to Bowring Bros. Ltd., St. John's, Newfoundland; 4.2.1906 wrecked at St. Shotts, on passage Cadiz to St. John's in ballast.

Anselm (1)
1882-1898
1,562
1882 built by A. Leslie and Company, Hebburn, for Booth; 1898 to W. A. Powell (W. Machea); 1901 to New Orleans, Belize Royal Mail and Central American Steamship Company (United Fruit Company); 1903 to Belize Mail and Transport Co. Ltd., Belize; 7.2.1908 stranded near Puerto Cortes, Honduras, refloated and towed to New York for breaking up.

Lanfranc (1)
1884-1898
1,657
1884 built by T. Royden and Sons, Liverpool, for Booth; 1898 to J. Montgomery, Belize, renamed *Olympia*; 1901 to Belize Mail and Transport Co. Ltd., Belize; 1907 to Cia Colonizadora de la Costa Oriental de Yucatan, Mexico; 1914 to New York and New Orleans Steamship Company, New York, renamed *Plan de Guadeloupe*; 1919 to Maru Navigation Company, New York, renamed *St. Charles*; 1923 broken up in the U.S.A.

Cyril (1)
1884-1897
1,190
1882 built by the London and Glasgow Company, as *Pacaxo* for Brazil Steamship Company; 1884 to Booth, renamed *Cyril*; 1897 to Empreza Navegacao Gram Para (F. Gomes and Company), Para, renamed *Braganca*; 1907 to Lloyd Brasileiro; 27.12.1925 wrecked off Aracari, on passage from Fort Aleza.

Gregory
1889-1897
1,498
1879 built by Schlesinger Davis and Company, Newcastle, as *Laurium* for Cie Maritime du Pacifique, Havre; 1889 to Booth, renamed *Gregory*; 1897 to Empreza Navegacao Gram Para (F. Gomes and Company), Para, renamed *Guajara*; 1907 to Lloyd Brasileiro; 1930 broken up.

Justin (1)
1890-1898
1,774
1880 built by Hall, Russell and Company, Aberdeen, as *Ponca* for Mediterranean and New York Steamship Company; 1890 to Booth, renamed *Justin*; 1898 to G. Beck, Dunkirk; 28.7.1905

Name and Period in Fleet	Gross Tons	History
		wrecked near Conquet, on passage Bilbao to Dunkirk.
Origen (1) 1890-1899	1,612	1886 built by Hall, Russell and Company, Aberdeen, as *Gloamin* for J. & R. Musie, Dundee; 1890 to Booth, renamed *Origen*; 1899 to Acties Origen (H. Waage), Christiania; 13.11.1915 left Philadelphia for Copenhagen and lost without trace.
Hilary (1) 1892-1905	1,930	1889 built by Thompson, Dundee, as *Red Sea* for Dundee, Perth and London Company; 1892 to Booth, renamed *Hilary*; 1905 to Rhederei Hilary GmbH (Sonder Wieler and Company), Cologne; 1911 to K. Fukagawa, Tsurumi, renamed *Misumi Maru*; 1916 to Towa Kisen K.K., Nishinomiya, renamed *Toryu Maru*; 1922 to Hashimoto Seitaro, Tsurumi; 1925 to Koike Goshi Kaisha, Susami; 1926 to Koryu Shoten Goshi Kaisha, Kobe; c1928 to Yamamoto Shoten Goshi Kaisha, Kobe; 2.5.1945 torpedoed and sunk West of Chemulpo.
Hildebrand (1) *Huayna* 1893-1917	1,988	1893 built by Hall, Russell and Company, Aberdeen, for Booth; 1908 to Iquitos, renamed *Huayna*; 1911 to Booth; 1917 to the Admiralty, and converted into a "Q" ship; 1919 to Dutrus y Carsi, Valencia, renamed *Manuel Carsi*; 19.5.1921 foundered off Cabo Torinana, on passage Gijon to Seville.
Hubert (1) *Atahualpa* 1894-1919	1,965	1894 built by Hall, Russell and Company, Aberdeen, for Booth; 1908 to Iquitos; renamed *Atahualpa*; 1911 to Booth; 1919 to Franco-British Steamship Company, renamed *City of Algiers*; 1922 to P. Messina, Catania, renamed *Vita Nova*; 1925 to Fr. Indelicato and Ci, Catania; 29.11.1927 foundered off Catania.
Dominic (1) 1895-1923	2,966	1895 built by Barclay, Curle and Company, Glasgow, for Booth; 1923 to C. M. Lemos and Company, Syra, renamed *Taxiarchis*; 1931 to Kalkavan Zade Riza ve Mahdumu Ismail (Vapur Sirketi), Istanbul, renamed *Nazim*; 13.12.1952 arrived at Grays for breaking up by T. W. Ward.
Horatio 1895-1911	3,212	1892 built by Edwards Shipbuilding Company, Newcastle, as *Horsley Tower* for F. Stumore and Company, London; 1893 to Wilson Line, Hull;

Name and Period in Fleet	Gross Tons	History

1894 renamed *Horatio*; 1895 to Booth; 1911 to C. Salvesen, Leith; 11.3.1916 lost by fire at Leith Harbour, South Georgia.

Dunstan (1)
1896-1923 — 2,994 — 1896 built by Barclay, Curle and Company, Glasgow, for Booth; 1923 to M. E. Kulukundis, Chios, renamed *Despina*; 12.9.1923 lost in collision with *Saxicava* off Gibraltar, on passage Swansea to Savona.

Polycarp (1)
1896-1912 — 3,003 — 1896 built by Barclay, Curle and Company, Glasgow, for Booth; 1912 to Rederi A/B Banco (C. J. Banck), Stockholm, renamed *Augusta*; 1918 to Rederi A/B Transatlantic (G. Carlsson), Gothenburg, renamed *Bia*; 1922 to Rederi A/B Bore (G. E. Sandstrom), Gothenburg, renamed *Falco*; 1935 to Parabrokarsko Drustvo S.O.I. "Alcesu", Orebic, renamed *Bosiljka*; 19.6.1942 torpedoed and sunk off New Orleans.

Augustine (2)
1896-1912 — 3,507 — 1879 built by Barclay, Curle and Company, Glasgow, as *Grantully Castle* for Donald Currie and Company; 1896 to Booth, renamed *Augustine*; 9.1912 broken up by Harris Bros., Falmouth.

Jerome (2)
1897-1911 — 2,923 — 1877 built by Napier and Sons, Glasgow, as *Warwick Castle* for Donald Currie and Company; 1897 to Booth, renamed *Jerome*; 1911 to the Turkish Government (Administration de Nav. a Vap. Ottomane), renamed *Kerasounde*; 1924 renamed *Kiresson*; 1926 broken up.

Benedict (1)
1897-1924 — 3,457 — 1894 built by Sir Raylton Dixon and Co. Ltd., Middlesbrough, as *Leyden* for Stoomvaart Maats "Leyden", Rotterdam; 1896 to Leyden Steamship Co. Ltd. (James H. Beazley), Liverpool; 1897 to Booth, renamed *Benedict*; 1924 to M. Vassiliades, Chios, renamed *Vassilios;* 1930 to G. M. Crussachi and Mme. Marie Olivier, Chios, renamed *Monarchis*; 1932 broken up in Italy.

Huascar
1898-1908 — 960 — 1896 built by Sunderland Shipbuilding Co. Ltd., Sunderland, as *Huascar* for Hernandez and Company, Liverpool; 1898 to Booth Iquitos; 1901 to Iquitos; 1908 to D. Tejero Perez, Coruna, renamed *Coruna*; 1918 to D. Arturo Cert., Coruna, renamed *Tibulado*; 1918 to Cia. Nav. Iturri (E. Goiri), renamed *Iturri-Azkar*; 1922 resold, renamed

Name and Period in Fleet	Gross Tons	History
		Japsis; 1930 to Bonifacio de Ajuria, Bilbao, renamed *Juli*; 20.3.1933 foundered West of Cabo Sardas.
Bolivar 1898-1909	1,016	1898 built by Hall, Russell and Co. Ltd., Aberdeen, for Booth Iquitos; 1901 to Iquitos; 1909 to Jose Pinto Quieros, Santos, renamed *Paulista*; 25.6.1913 wrecked off Paraty, on passage Santos to Rio de Janeiro.
Basil (2) 1898-1917	3,223	1895 built by Workman, Clark and Co. Ltd., Belfast, as *Mourne* for Dixon and Sons, Belfast; 1898 to Booth, renamed *Basil*; 11.11.1917 lost in collision with steamer *Margaux* in the English Channel, South East of Owers Light Vessel.
Bernard (2) 1898-1911	3,280	1895 built by Workman, Clark and Co. Ltd., Belfast, as *Mount Sirion* for Smith and Service, Glasgow; 1898 to Booth, renamed *Bernard*; 1911 to H. & C. Grayson, renamed *Redbarn*; 1911 to A. A. Embiricos, Andros, renamed *Lordos Byron*; 5.11.1911 foundered off the Casquets, on passage Theodosia to Antwerp.
Gregory (2) 1899-1920	2,030	1891 built by Palmer and Company, Newcastle, as *Cresswell* for J. E. Bowser and Sons, Newcastle; 1899 to Booth, renamed *Gregory*; 1907 to Iquitos; 1911 to Booth; 22.11.1920 wrecked on Tutoia Bar, on passage New York to Manaos.
Clement (2) 1900-1914	3,445	1896 built by Napier and Sons, Glasgow, as *La Plata* for Royal Mail Steam Packet Company. 1900 to Booth, renamed *Clement*; 1914 to Lawrence Smith, Montreal, renamed *Freshfield*; 5.8.1918 torpedoed and sunk in Mediterranean, off Cape Colonne.
Lisbonense 1901-1904	1,657	See Appendix 2 for details.
Paraense 1901-1902	1,697	See Appendix 2 for details.
Sobralense 1901-1904	1,982	See Appendix 2 for details.
Obidense 1901-1910	2,380	See Appendix 2 for details.
Grangense 1901-1910	2,162	See Appendix 2 for details.

Name and Period in Fleet	Gross Tons	History
Cametense 1901-1909	2,184	See Appendix 2 for details.
Fluminense 1901-1909	2,154	See Appendix 2 for details.
Madeirense 1901-1910	2,831	See Appendix 2 for details.
Napo 1901-1913	1,091	See Appendix 2 for details.
Ucayali 1901-1914	1,052	See Appendix 2 for details.
Javary 1901-1914	1,249	See Appendix 2 for details.
Maranhense 1901-1910	2,767	See Appendix 2 for details.
Amazonense 1901-1911	2,828	See Appendix 2 for details.
Cearense 1901-1911	2,769	See Appendix 2 for details.
Cyril (2) 1902-1905	4,380	1883 built by John Elder and Company, Glasgow, as *Howarden Castle* for Castle Mail Steam Packet Co. Ltd. (Donald Currie and Company), London; 1900 to Union Castle Line; 1902 to Booth, renamed *Cyril*; 5.9.1905 lost in collision with *Anselm* (2) in River Amazon, below Para.
Ambrose 1903-1915	4,595	1903 built by Sir Raylton Dixon and Co. Ltd., Middlesbrough, for Booth; 10.12.1914 requisitioned by the Admiralty—converted into an Armed Merchant Cruiser—H.M.S. *Ambrose*; 1915 to the Admiralty and later converted into a Submarine Depot ship; 1938 renamed H.M.S. *Cochrane*; 1946 broken up by T. W. Ward, Inverkeithing.
Justin (2) 1904-1930	3,809	1904 built by Barclay, Curle and Co. Ltd., Glasgow, for Booth; 1930 broken up by N.V. de Koophandel, Neuwlekkerland, Holland.
Boniface (1) 1904-1917	3,799	1904 built by Barclay, Curle and Co. Ltd., Glasgow, for Booth; 23.8.1917 torpedoed and sunk off Aran Islands.

Name and Period in Fleet	Gross Tons	History
Anselm (2) 1905-1922	5,450	1905 built by Workman, Clark and Co. Ltd., Belfast, for Booth; 1922 to Argentine owners, renamed *Commodoro Rivadavia*; 1942 to Argentine Government; 1944 renamed *Rio Santa Cruz*; 1959 broken up at Rio de Janeiro.
Cuthbert (1) 1906-1931	3,846	1906 built by R. & W. Hawthorn, Leslie and Co. Ltd., Hebburn, for Booth; 1931 broken up at La Spezia.
Crispin (1) 1907-1917	3,965	1907 built by Sir Raylton Dixon and Co. Ltd., Middlesbrough, for Booth; 29.3.1917 torpedoed and sunk off Hook Point, Waterford.
Antony (1) 1907-1917	6,446	1907 built by R. & W. Hawthorn, Leslie and Co. Ltd., Hebburn, for Booth; 17.3.1917 torpedoed and sunk off Coningbeg Light Vessel.
Lanfranc (2) 1907-1917	6,287	1907 built by Caledon Shipbuilding and Engineering Co. Ltd., Dundee, for Booth; 1914 fitted out as a hospital ship; 17.4.1917 torpedoed and sunk 4 miles N.E. of Havre.
Port Fairy 1907-1909	2,581	1887 built by Wigham Richardson and Company, Newcastle, as *Port Fairy* for William Milburn; 1892 to J. H. Andresen, Oporto, renamed *Dona Maria*; 1907 to Booth, renamed *Port Fairy*; 1909 to shipbreakers, but resold to Ellerman Lines for further trading and renamed *Italian*; 1913 broken up by T. W. Ward, Preston.
Manco 1908-1921	1,988	1908 built by Scott's Shipbuilding and Engineering Co. Ltd., Greenock, for Iquitos; 1911 to Booth; 1914-18 served as a Royal Fleet Auxiliary; 1921 to Vaccaro Bros. Steamship Company, Ceiba, Honduras, renamed *Morazan*; 1920s to American Fruit and Steamship Corp. (Standard Fruit and Steamship Corp.), Ceiba; 1930s to Seaboard Steamship Corp. (Standard Fruit and Steamship Corp.); 12.1941 while under Panamanian flag, captured by the Japanese at Shanghai; 1943 renamed *Ekkai Maru*; 8.9.1944 bombed and sunk in Colon Bay, S.W. of Manila.
Hilary (2) 1908-1917	6,329	1908 built by Caledon Shipbuilding and Engineering Co. Ltd., Dundee, for Booth; 7.12.1914 requisitioned by the Admiralty—converted into an Armed Merchant Cruiser—H.M.S. *Hilary*;

Name and Period in Fleet	Gross Tons	History
		25.5.1917 torpedoed and sunk West of the Shetland Islands.
Francis 1910-1931	3,963	1910 built by Barclay, Curle and Co. Ltd., Glasgow, for Booth; 1931 to Moller Line, renamed *Rosalie Moller*; 8.10.1941 sunk by air attack at Suez; after the war, raised and broken up.
Hubert (2) 1910-1934	3,946	1910 built by Barclay, Curle and Co. Ltd., Glasgow, for Booth; 1934 broken up by J. J. King, Troon.
Vincent (1) 1910-1912	986	1910 built by Mackie, Thompson and Co. Ltd., Glasgow, for Booth—special heavy lift ship for handling materials for Brazilian Railways; 1912 to Cia Zamorense de Nav. S.A. de Gutierrez Zamora, Santa Cruz, renamed *Libertad*; 3.8.1916 foundered off Cape San Antonio, Cuba.
Christopher 1910-1914	4,416	1910 built by Tyne Iron Shipbuilding Co. Ltd., Newcastle, for Booth; 1914 to Elder Dempster and Co. Ltd., Liverpool, renamed *Obuasi*; 8.7.1917 torpedoed and sunk 290 miles West of the Fastnet.
Stephen 1910-1934	4,444	1910 built by R. & W. Hawthorn, Leslie and Co. Ltd., Hebburn, for Booth; 15.12.1934 arrived at Briton Ferry for breaking up by T. W. Ward.
Denis (1) 1911-1932	4,435	1911 built by R. & W. Hawthorn, Leslie and Co. Ltd., Hebburn, for Booth; 1932 broken up by S.A. Cantiere di Portovenere, La Spezia.
Pancras 1911-1932	4,436	1911 built by R. & W. Hawthorn, Leslie and Co., Ltd., Hebburn, for Booth; 1932 broken up by S.A. Cantiere di Portovenere, La Spezia.
Aidan 1911-1936	4,545	1911 built by Tyne Iron Shipbuilding Co. Ltd., Newcastle, for Booth; 1936 broken up at Savona.
Hildebrand (2) 1911-1934	6,995	1911 built by Scott's Shipbuilding and Engineering Co. Ltd., Greenock, for Booth; 5.12.1914 requisitioned by the Admiralty—converted into an Armed Merchant Cruiser—H.M.S. *Hildebrand*, later on other Naval duties; 17.1.1919 returned to Booth; 1934 broken up by J. Cashmore, Newport.
Ceara 1911	437	1911 built by Cammell, Laird and Co. Ltd., Birkenhead; laid down for Booth, but before completion to G. A. Miranda Filho, Para; 1927 omitted from register, no other details.

Name and Period in Fleet	Gross Tons	History
Vincent (2) 1913	4,561	1895 built by Armstrong, Mitchell and Co. Ltd., Newcastle, as *Fort Salisbury* for British and Colonial Steam Navigation Co. Ltd. (Bucknall Bros.), London; 1900 transferred to Bucknall Steamship Lines Ltd. (Bucknall Bros.), London; 1913 to Booth, renamed *Vincent*; 1913 to Bank Line Ltd. (Andrew Weir and Company), renamed *Gujarat*; 1919 to H.M.H. Nemazee, Hong Kong; 1921 renamed *Gorjistan*; 1923 to Oriental Navigation Co. Ltd., Hong Kong; 1926 to H.M.H. Nemazee, Hong Kong; 5.10.1928 arrived at Kobe for breaking up by Borg and Co. Ltd.
Michael 1914-1924	3,172	1914 built by Sir Raylton Dixon and Co. Ltd., Middlesbrough, for Booth; 1924 to Algeria, renamed *Charles Schiaffino*; 1.2.1929 wrecked near Cape Villano, on passage Dunkirk to Algiers.
Alban (1) 1914-1935	5,223	1914 built by Caledon Shipbuilding and Engineering Co. Ltd., Dundee, for Booth; 5.1935 to shipbreakers at Genoa, but in 1936 resold for further trading to Ugo Musso, Genoa; 10.10.1941 damaged by air attack off Kerkena; 11.10.1941 torpedoed and sunk South of Lampedusa.
Oswald 1915-1917	5,185	1915 built by Sir Raylton Dixon and Co. Ltd., Middlesbrough, for Booth; 23.4.1917 torpedoed and sunk 200 miles S.W. of the Fastnet.
Origen (2) 1918	3,545	1918 built by Caledon Shipbuilding and Engineering Co. Ltd., Dundee, for Booth; 30.6.1918 torpedoed and sunk 115 miles S.W. of Ushant, outward bound on her maiden voyage.
Polycarp (2) 1918-1940	3,577	1918 built by Barclay, Curle and Co. Ltd., Glasgow, for Booth; 1939 to Board of Trade (Merchant Shipping Reserve), management allocated to Booth; 2.6.1940 torpedoed and sunk N.W. of Ushant.
Dominic (2) 1927-1932	3,396	1922 built by Krupps, Kiel, as *Nord Friesland* for Flensburger Dampfer GmbH (H. Schuldt), Flensburg; 1923 to H. C. Horn, Flensburg, renamed *Claus Horn*; 1927 to Booth, renamed *Dominic*; 6.1932 to Etabl Maurel and Prom, Bordeaux, renamed *Montesquieux*; 12.1942 taken over by Italy, renamed *Enna*; 30.5.1943 sunk by air attack at Naples; 1947 raised and broken up at Naples.

Name and Period in Fleet	Gross Tons	History
Basil (3) 1928-1950	4,873	1928 built by R. & W. Hawthorn, Leslie and Co. Ltd., Hebburn, for Booth; 1950 to Parthenon Shipping Co. S.A., (Faros Shipping Company), Panama, renamed *Parthenon*; 21.5.1951 grounded near Vizagapatam, on passage Calcutta to Bombay; 21.9.1951 still aground, caught fire and burnt out; total loss.
Boniface (2) 1928-1949	4,877	1928 built by R. & W. Hawthorn, Leslie and Co. Ltd., Hebburn, for Booth; 1949 to Lamport & Holt renamed *Browning*; 1951 to Cia de Nav. Niques, Panama, renamed *Sannicola*; 1951 to Muko Kisen K.K., Japan, renamed *Mizuho Maru*; 28.2.1961 arrived at Mukaishima for breaking up.
Benedict (2) 1930-1948	4,920	1930 built by Cammell, Laird and Co. Ltd., Birkenhead, for Booth; 1948 to Lamport & Holt, renamed *Bronte*; 1950 to Turkish owners, renamed *Muzaffer*; 1957 resold, renamed *Umran*; 14.2.1961 arrived at Vigo for breaking up.
Hilary (3) 1931-1959	7,403	1931 built by Cammell, Laird and Co. Ltd., Birkenhead, for Booth; 15.9.1959 arrived at Inverkeithing for breaking up by T. W. Ward Ltd.
Clement (3) 1934-1939	5,051	1934 built by Cammell, Laird and Co. Ltd., Birkenhead, for Booth; 30.9.1939 sunk by the *Admiral Graf Spee* S.E. of Pernambuco.
Crispin (2) 1934-1941	5,051	1934 built by Cammell, Laird and Co. Ltd., Birkenhead, for Booth; 8.1940 requisitioned by the Admiralty as an Ocean Boarding Vessell; 3.1.1941 torpedoed in the North Atlantic, and sank the following day.
Anselm (3) 1935-1941	5,954	1935 built by W. Denny and Bros., Dumbarton, for Booth; 1.1940 converted to a troopship; 5.7.1941 torpedoed and sunk 300 miles North of the Azores.
Dunstan (2) 1935-1941	5,149	1925 built by Duncan and Co. Ltd., Glasgow, as *Saint Oswald* for Rankin Gilmour and Co. Ltd., Liverpool; 1929 to Cie Francaise d'Armement et d'Importation de Nitrate de Soude, Dunkirk, renamed *A.D. Bordes*; 1935 to Booth, renamed *Dunstan*; 6.4.1941 sunk by air attack N.W. of Cape Wrath.

Hubert (3) *Cuthbert* (2) 1946-1953	4,115	1946 built by Wm. Pickersgill and Sons Ltd., Sunderland; laid down for the Ministry of War Transport, but completed as *Hubert* for Booth; 1951 renamed *Cuthbert*; 1953 to Austasia, renamed *Mandama*; 1965 to Mouzakies Ltda. S.A., renamed *Loucia N*; 26.11.1970 arrived at Shanghai for breaking up.
Bernard (3) 1946-1947	6,902	1940 built by Barclay, Curle and Co. Ltd., Glasgow, as *Empire Voice* for the Ministry of War Transport, managers—British India Steam Navigation Co. Ltd.; 1943 managers changed to Booth; 1946 to Booth, renamed *Bernard*; 1947 to L + H, renamed *Byron*; 1953 renamed *Lalande*; 1961 to Wm. Brandt, Sons and Company, renamed *Uncle Bart*; 8.9.1961 arrived at Moji for breaking up.
Pachitea *Dunstan* (4) 1946-1958	3,831	1945 built by Leatham D. Smith Shipbuilding Corp., Sturgeon Bay, Wisconsin; launched as *Tulare* for the United States Navy, but completed as *Coastal Challenger* for United States Maritime Commission; 1946 to Panama Shipping Corp., bareboat chartered to Booth, renamed *Pachitea*; 1954 to Booth, renamed *Dunstan*; 1958 to L + H, renamed *Sallust*; 1959 to Austasia, renamed *Malacca*; 1962 to Kie Hock Shipping Company, Hong Kong, renamed *Tong Hong*; 25.10.1967 sailed from Kawasaki for Singapore and lost without trace.
Jutahay 1946-1954	3,843	1945 built by Walter Butler Shipbuilders Inc., Duluth, Minn., as *Frank J. Petrarco* for United States Maritime Commission; 1946 to Panama Shipping Corp., bareboat chartered to Booth, renamed *Jutahay*; 1954 to L + H, renamed *Sargent*, and registered at Port of Spain, Trinidad; 1962 to A. Halcoussis, Greece, renamed *Pamit*; 1966 to Bambero Cia Nav. S.A., Liberia, renamed *Bambero*; 3.3.1970 arrived at Castellon for breaking up by I. M. Varela Davalillo.
Dominic (3) 1947-1961	3,860	1945 built by Consolidated Steel Corp., Wilmington, California, as *Hickory Stream* for United States Maritime Commission; 1947 to Booth, renamed *Dominic*; 1961 to Guan Guan Ltd., renamed *Samodra Mas*; 1964 to Hong Kong South

Name and Period in Fleet	Gross Tons	History

Sea Shipping Co. Ltd., Hong Kong, renamed *Lombardus*; 1965 renamed *Golden Ocean*; 1970 transferred to Singapore flag; 1970 to Thio Keng Leng, Mogadishu; 3.6.1971 foundered off Andaman Islands.

Dunstan (3)
Basil (5)
1948-1951
1958-1969 — 2,993 — 1948 built by Wm. Pickersgill and Sons Ltd., Sunderland, for Booth; 1951 to L + H, renamed *Sallust*; 1958 to Booth, renamed *Dunstan*; 1966 renamed *Basil*; 1968 to Cia. Mtma. Viahoulis S.A., Panama, renamed *Christina*; 3.1.1969 badly damaged by fire at Galveston; 1969 broken up at Barranquilla.

Denis (2)
1949-1968 — 2,990 — 1949 built by Wm. Pickersgill and Sons Ltd., Sunderland, for Booth; 1968 to Vasmanto Shipping Co. S.A., Liberia, renamed *Akrogiali*; 1972 broken up at Piraeus.

Hildebrand (3)
1951-1957 — 7,735 — 1951 built by Cammell, Laird and Co. Ltd., Birkenhead, for Booth; 25.9.1957 wrecked near Cascais, Portugal, on voyage Liverpool to Brazil via Lisbon; 28.10.1957 salvage abandoned.

Crispin (3)
Dunstan (5)
1951-1953
1966 — 4,472 — 1951 built by Wm. Pickersgill and Sons Ltd., Sunderland, for Booth; 1953 to Austasia, renamed *Mandowi*; 1966 to Booth, renamed *Dunstan*; 1966 bareboat chartered to L + H, renamed *Rubens*; 1973 to George Kalogeras, Piraeus, renamed *Irini K*; 24.4.1974 arrived at Istanbul for breaking up.

Vianna
1951-1955 — 2,825 — 1943 built by St. John Drydock and Shipbuilding Co. Ltd., St. John, N.B., as *Rockwood Park* for Park Steamship Co. of Canada Ltd., Montreal; later renamed *La Grande Hermine*; 1951 to Panama Shipping Corp., bareboat chartered to Booth, renamed *Vianna*; 1955 to Arm. L. Mazzella and Cie., Oran, renamed *Cap Falcon*; 1963 to Emilio Parrello, Naples, renamed *Licola*; 1971 broken up at Spezia.

Clement (4)
Benedict (3)
1953
1966-1967 — 4,300 — 1953 built by Wm. Pickersgill and Sons Ltd., Sunderland; laid down as *Clement* for Booth, launched as *Malay Star* for BSL, completed as *Malay* for Austasia; 1964 renamed *Mahsuri*; 1966 to Booth, renamed *Benedict*; 1967 bareboat chartered to L + H, renamed *Renoir*; 1971 to Starlight Steamship Co. S.A., Panama, renamed *Diamond Star*; 1973 broken up at Suao, Taiwan.

Name and Period in Fleet	Gross Tons	History
Drover 1954	1,463	1923 built by Caledon Shipbuilding and Engineering Co. Ltd., Dundee, as *Copeland* for Clyde Shipping Co. Ltd., Glasgow; 1946 to G. Heyn and Sons Ltd., Belfast, renamed *North Down*; 1954 to Union International Co. Ltd., managers—Booth, registered at Belfast and renamed *Drover*; 1954 to Belfast Steamship Co. Ltd., renamed *Ulster Herdsman*; 5.10.1963 arrived at Passage West, Cork, for breaking up.
Vamos 1954-1968	1,090	1952 built by Glommens Mek. Verks., Fredrikstad, as *Vamos* for Sverre Ditlev-Simonsen and Company, Oslo; 1954 to Panama Shipping Corp., bareboat chartered to Booth; c1964 lengthened, gross tonnage increased to 1,700; 1968 to Rapier and Ray Navigation Co. Ltd., Panama, renamed *Defiance*; 28.6.1969 foundered 270 miles South of Lima, in position 16.10S, 75.46W, on passage Antofagasta to Callao.
Hubert (4) 1955-1964	8,062	1955 built by Cammell, Laird and Co. Ltd., Birkenhead, for Booth; 1964 to BSL, bareboat chartered to Austasia, renamed *Malaysia*; 1976 to Atlas Shipping Agency (U.K.) Ltd. (Gulfeast Ship Management Ltd.), Singapore, converted to a cattle carrier and renamed *Khalij Express*; 1976 to Halena Shipping Co. Ltd. (Gulfeast Shipping Pte. Ltd.), Singapore; 1981 to Arabian Maritime Transport Co. Ltd. (Gulfeast Shipping Pte. Ltd.), Saudi Arabia; 1981 managers discontinued; 1984 broken up at Port Alang, India by N.C.K. Exports and Sons Pvt. Ltd.
Veloz (1) 1955-1967	1,312	1955 built by Norderwerft Koser and Mayer, Hamburg, for Booth; 1965 lengthened, gross tonnage increased to 1,607; 1967 to Linea Amazonica S.A. Callao, renamed *Atahalpa*; 1976 to Queen Sea Marine Co. Ltd., Cyprus, renamed *Falcon* 1; still in service.
Crispin (4) 1956-1974	1,593	1956 built by T. van Duivendijk Scheepswerf N.V., Lekkerkerk, for Booth; 1964 lengthened, gross tonnage increased to 1,816; 1974 to Armasol Line, El Salvador, renamed *Ana*; still in service.
Venimos 1956-1973	1,309	1856 built by Norderwerft Koser and Mayer, Hamburg, for Salient Shipping Co. (Bermuda)

Name and Period in Fleet	Gross Tons	History

Ltd., Hamilton, bareboat chartered to Booth; 1964 lengthened, gross tonnage increased to 1,607; 1973 to Compania Nationale de Nav. S.A. (Navenal), Bogota, renamed *Acaima*; still in service.

Viajero 1957-1973   1,204   1957 built by Norderwerft Koser and Mayer, Hamburg, for Panama Shipping Corp., bareboat chartered to Booth; 1964 lengthened, gross tonnage increased to 1,476; 1973 to Compania Nationale de Nav. S.A. (Navenal), Bogota, renamed *Pigonza*; still in service.

Vigilante 1958-1968   915   1955 built by Schiffsw. A. Pahl, Hamburg, as *Montrose* for Buries Marks; 1958 to L + H, bareboat chartered to Booth, renamed *Vigilante*; 1968 to Cunningham Navigation Co. Ltd., Nassau, renamed *Caribbean Mara*; 28.2.1974 abandoned on fire in position 26.35N, 86.42W, on passage Mobile to Santo Domingo.

Clement (5) 1959-1979   1,565   1959 built by T. van Duivendijk Scheepswerf N.V., Lekkerkerk, for Booth; 1964 lengthened, gross tonnage increased to 1,902; 1979 to Dalin Maritime Corp., Monrovia, renamed *Element*; still in service.

Basil (4) 1960-1964   3,022   1939 built by Burmeister and Wain, Copenhagen, as *Mosdale* for A/S Mosvold Shipping, Norway; 1954 to BSL, renamed *Albion Star*; 1954 to L + H, renamed *Balzac*; 1959 renamed *Carroll*; 1960 to B.S.L., renamed *Norman Star*; 1960 bareboat chartered to Booth, renamed *Basil*; 1964 to H. and D. Kyriakos, Greece, renamed *Eleni K*; 1966 to Helen Shipping Corp. (Panama) Ltd., Greece, renamed *Eleni Kyriakou*; 1970 renamed *Olga*; 1970 to Kreta Shipping Co. S.A., Greece, renamed *Georgios Markakis*; 1973 to Amarinthos Shipping Co. Ltd., Cyprus, renamed *Nikos S*; 4.5.1973 arrived at Bilbao for breaking up.

Bede 1961-1963   3,111   1938 built by Burmeister and Wain, Copenhagen, as *Barfleur* for Cie Generale d'Armement Maritime, France; 1955 to BSL, 1955 to L + H, renamed *Boswell*; 1960 renamed *Crome*; 1960 to BSL, renamed *Roman Star*; 1961 bareboat chartered to Booth, renamed *Bede*; 1963 to Rahcassi Shipping

Name and Period in Fleet	Gross Tons	History

Co. S.A., Greece, renamed *Victoria Elena*; 16.1.1967 caught fire while loading a cargo of cotton at Thessalonika, Greece; 19.1.1967 beached in a heavily damaged condition off Piraeus, declared a Constructive Total Loss, refloated; 1967 broken up at La Spezia by Lotti S.p.A.

Anselm (4)
1961-1963
10,854 1950 built by John Cockerill S.A., Hoboken, Belgium, as *Baudouinville* for Compagnie Maritime Belge (Lloyd Royal) Soc. Anon. (Agence Maritime Internationale S.A.), Antwerp; 1957 renamed *Thysville*; 1961 to Booth, renamed *Anselm*; 1963 to BSL, renamed *Iberia Star*; 1965 bareboat chartered to Austasia, renamed *Australasia*; 1972 to Euroasia Carriers Ltd., Singapore; 1972 to Chou's Iron and Steel (Industrial) Co. Ltd., Taiwan, for breaking up at Hualien.

Valiente
Veloz (2)
1961-1973
1,312 1959 built by Norderwerft Koser and Mayer, Hamburg, as *Spenser* for L + H; 1961 to Panama Shipping Corp., bareboat chartered to Booth, renamed *Valiente*; 1964 lengthened, gross tonnage increased to 1,609; 1969 renamed *Veloz*; 1973 to Compania Nationale de Nav. S.A. (Navenal), Bogota, renamed *Tanambi*; 23.8.1979 grounded in Panama Canal, while on passage Bueno Ventura to Guanta; subsequently refloated; 2.12.1982 arrived at Cartagena, Colombia, for breaking up.

Veras
1962-1973
1,282 1959 built by Geo. Brown Ltd., Greenock, as *Siddons* for L + H, (originally laid down for BSL); 1962 bareboat chartered to Booth, renamed *Veras*; 1966 lengthened at Hamburg, gross tonnage increased to 1,616; 1973 to Chania Cia. Nav. S.A., Panama, renamed *Kydonia*; 1976 to Fayrouz Cia. Nav. S.A., Panama, renamed *Fayrouz*; 4.10.1978 damaged by fire at Piraeus, repaired and still in service.

Boniface
(3)
1963-1967
1970-1974
4,693 1956 built by Wm. Pickersgill and Sons Ltd., Sunderland, as *Rossetti* for L + H; 1963 bareboat chartered to Booth, renamed *Boniface*; 1967 charter ended, renamed *Rossetti*; 1970 to Booth, renamed *Boniface*; 1974 to Hydra Navigation Co. Ltd., Greece, renamed *Amaryllis*; 1978 to Imerama S.A., Greece, renamed *Zefyros*; 1979 broken up at Kaohsiung.

Name and Period in Fleet	Gross Tons	History
Bernard (4) 1965-1967 1970-1974	4,459	1952 built by Wm. Pickersgill and Sons Ltd., Sunderland, as *Siddons* for L + H; 1955 renamed *Rubens*; 1965 bareboat chartered to Booth, renamed *Bernard*; 1967 charter ended, renamed *Rossini*; 1970 to Booth, renamed *Bernard*; 1973 to Sopac Bulk Carriers Co. Inc., Panama, renamed *Berwell Adventure*; 1974 to Booth; 1974 to Overseas Marine Corp., Panama; 1974 to Kelsey Bay Shipping Co. Ltd., Panama, renamed *Al Turab*; 1978 broken up at Gadani Beach.
Cyril (3) 1967-1978	1,849	1961 built by T. van Duijvendijk Scheepswerf N.V., Lekkerkerk, as *Sheridan* for Booth, bareboat chartered to L + H; 1964 to L + H; 1964 lengthened at Smith's Dock Co. Ltd., North Shields, gross tonnage increased from 1,535; 1967 bareboat chartered to Booth, renamed *Cyril*; 1973 to Panama Shipping Corp., bareboat chartered to Booth; 1978 to Altis Shipping Co. S.A., Greece, renamed *Angie*; 1979 to Ocean Breeze Cia. Nav. S.A., Greece; 1980 to Aegaeus Maritime Co. S.A., Greece, renamed *Amalia*; 1981 to Wes Line Co. Ltd., Panama, renamed *West Point*; 1985 to Perkapalan Sri Tomah Sendirian Berhad, Malaysia, renamed *Tumoh Saty*; still in service.
Cuthbert 1967-1977	1,869	1962 built by T. van Duijvendijk Scheepswerf N.V., Lekkerkerk, as *Spenser* for Booth, bareboat chartered to L + H; 1964 lengthened at Smith's Dock Co. Ltd., North Shields, tonnage increased from 1,549; 1964 to L + H; 1967 bareboat chartered to Booth, renamed *Cuthbert*; 1973 to Panama Shipping Corp., bareboat chartered to Booth; 1977 to Associated Levant Lines S.A.L., Lebanon, renamed *Barouk*; 1982 to Naviera An Hing S. de R.L., Vanuatu, renamed *An Hing*; still in service.
Dominic (4) 1967-1975	3,324	1953 built by Aalborg Vaerft A/S, Aalborg, as *Jonna Dan* for Rederi 'Ocean' A/S (J. Lauritzen), Copenhagen; 1964 to Austasia, renamed *Makati*; 1967 to Booth, renamed *Dominic*, and lengthened at Hoboken, increasing her gross tonnage to 4,584; 1975 to Ring Shipping Co. Ltd. (Sinergasia Shipbrokers Ltd.), Cyprus, renamed *Dominica*; 1976 to Carl Shipping Enterprises Corp. (Meridian Shipping Enterprises Ltd.), Greece, renamed *Trojan*; 1981 to Nikki Maritime Ltd., Panama,

Name and Period in Fleet	Gross Tons	History
		renamed *Ragnar*; 18.9.1982 abandoned by her crew in position 32.52N, 47.25W, after her engineroom had flooded during a voyage from Cuba to Libya with a cargo of cement.
Ambrose (3) (chartered) 1974-1976	2,992	Singapore flag motorship *Dollart* (1971) time chartered from 9.4.1974 to 22.5.1976 (12 round voyages) and renamed *Ambrose* for the period.
Antony (2) (chartered) 1974-1977	3,062	West German flag motorship *Bilstein* (1967) time chartered from 1.5.1974 to 7.4.1977 (16 round voyages) and renamed *Antony* for the period.
Alban (2) 1976-1978	4,547	1971 built by Schiffswerft Neptun, Rostock, as *Lyra* for D/S A/S Laly (C.T. Gogstad), Oslo; 1976 to Booth, renamed *Alban*; 9.1978 to Nan Yang Shipping Company, Macam, Port of Registry— Canton, renamed *Lin Jiang*; still in service.
Benedict (4) 1979-1986	3,636	1979 built by EMAQ—Engenharia e Maquinas S.A., Rio de Janeiro for Booth; 1986 to Losinjska Plovidba Oour Brodarstvo, (Venisol Shipping Corp., Panama), Rijeka, Yugoslavia, renamed *Zamet*; still in service.
Boniface (4) 1979-1986	3,636	1979 built by EMAQ—Engenharia e Maquinas S.A., Rio de Janeiro for Booth; 1986 to Losinjska Plovidba Oour Brodarsvtvo, Rijeka, renamed *Pecine*; still in service.
Clement (6) (chartered) 1986-	3,986	Dutch flag motorship *Frisian Glory* (1985) time chartered from 1986 and renamed *Clement*; present fleet.
Crispin (5) (chartered) 1986-	3,986	Dutch flag motorship *Frisian Hope* (1985) time chartered from 1986 and renamed *Crispin*; present fleet.

13. APPENDIX TWO
RED CROSS LINE—FLEET LIST

Name and Period in Fleet	Gross Tons	History
Paraense (1) 1869-1870	1,300	1869 built by T. Royden and Sons, Liverpool, for Singlehurst; 4.5.1870 wrecked at Ceara.
Maranhense (1) 1869-1880	1,334	1869 built by T. Royden and Sons, Liverpool, for Singlehurst; 1880 to T. R. Oswald, Liverpool; 1882 to Italy, renamed *Camilla*; 1887 to L. Scorcia and Figli, Bari, renamed *Europa*; 1898 to Idarei Massousieh, Constantinople, renamed *Shark*; 1912 broken up.
Cearense (1) 1869-1899	1,381	1869 built by T. Royden and Sons, Liverpool, for Singlehurst; 1899 to T. and V. Flores, Palermo, renamed *Picnic*; 1900 to Soc. Meridionale de Transport, Palermo; 1902 broken up at Palermo.
Lisbonense 1871-1901	1,657	1871 built by T. Royden and Sons, Liverpool, for Singlehurst; 1888 re-engined; 1901 to Booth; 1904 to Vaccaro Bros., Liverpool, renamed *Joseph Vaccaro; 1916 to Cuyamel Fruit Company, Puerto Cortez, renamed Quimstan*; 19.8.1929 abandoned on fire in North Atlantic, on passage Norfolk, Va. to Genoa.
Paraense (2) 1871-1901	1,697	1871 built by T. Royden and Sons, Liverpool, for Singlehurst; 1901 to Booth; 1902 to Vaccaro Bros. Steamship Company, Ceiba, Honduras, renamed *Rosina*; 1916 to Cuyamel Fruit Company, Puerto Cortez, renamed *Omoa*; 1926 broken up.
Amazonense (1) 1879-1881	1,865	1879 built at Southampton for Singlehurst; 16.4.1881 wrecked off St. David's Head, on voyage Liverpool to Para, via Havre.
Theresina 1880-1898	1,145	1876 built as *Theresina* for W. Dodd, Liverpool; 1880 to Singlehurst; 1898 to Palgrave Murphy, Dublin; 1899 renamed *City of Brussels*; 1922 to A. Gibaldi di F., Empedocle, renamed *C. F. Gibaldi*; 31.10.1925 wrecked at Zuetina.

Name and Period in Fleet	Gross Tons	History
Amazonense (2) 1881-1896	1,692	1869 built by Wigham Richardson and Company, Newcastle, as *Hindostan* for Apcar and Company; 1881 to Singlehurst, renamed *Amazonense*; 1896 to J. H. Tandonnet Freres, Bordeaux, renamed *Saint Augustin*; 23.7.1897 put into Cartagena with boiler trouble; 9.1897 broken up at Marseilles.
Maranhense (2) 1881-1895	1,480	1880 built by Sunderland Shipbuilding Company, Sunderland, as *Blodwen* for Arvon Shipping Company, Caernarvon, ship registered at Liverpool; 1882 to Singlehurst, renamed *Maranhense*; 1895 to J. H. Tandonnet Freres, Bordeaux, renamed *Saint Antoine*; 1902 to L. Flornoy et Fils, Nantes; 1907 to Queenstown Dry Docks, Shipbuilding and Engineering Company, Queenstown, renamed *Maranhense*; 1908 to Palgrave Murphy and Company, Dublin, renamed *City of Cork*; 1918 to Williams Bros., Hull; 1925 broken up by T. W. Ward Ltd., Inverkeithing.
Manauense 1883-1898	1,672	1874 built by J. Reid and Company, Port Glasgow, as *Bowen* for Eastern and Australian Steamship Company; 1883 to Singlehurst, renamed *Manauense*; 1898 to T. T. Edwards, Liverpool; 1899 to D. Bruse and Company, Dundee; 1900 to La Compania Mexicana de Navegacion S.A., Vera Cruz, renamed *Mexico*; 1901 to British Columbia Steamship Co. Ltd., Vancouver, renamed *Manauense*; 1902 to B. H. Michaelsen, St. Thomas, Danish West Indies; 16.12.1903 stranded off Muroran, on passage Hakodate to San Francisco. Total loss.
Portuense 1883-1890	1,470	1875 built by Aitken and Mansell, Glasgow, as *Abdiel* for Richard Blythe, London; 1880 to Merchant Steamship Co. Ltd., Liverpool, renamed *Glenapp*; 1883 to Singlehurst, renamed *Portuense*; 28.8.1890 foundered near Angada, 250 miles from Bahamas, on passage Baltimore to Para.
Sobralense 1884-1901	1,982	1884 built by Barrow Shipbuilding Co. Ltd., Barrow, for Singlehurst; 1901 to Booth; 1904 to Lee Li Chien, Hong Kong; 12.5.1905 mined and sunk off Port Arthur, on passage Newchang to Kobe.

72

Name and Period in Fleet	Gross Tons	History
Grangense (1) 1887-1890	420	1887 built by Barrow Shipbuilding Co. Ltd., Barrow, for Singlehurst; 1890 to Cia de Estrade de Ferro de Bahia e Minas, Rio de Janeiro, renamed *Augusto Leal*; 1898 to Velhote Silva e Cie, Para, renamed *Parnahyba*; 1913 to Banco do Para, Para; 1914 to J. A. da Silva Padreira, Para; 1922 broken up.
Carvoeira 1887-1901	1,356	Sailing ship. 1869 built by T. Royden and Sons, Liverpool, as *Locksley Hall* for R. Alexander, Liverpool; 1881 to Lowden Edgar and Company, Liverpool; 1887 to Singlehurst, renamed *Carvoeira*; and converted to a hulk on the Amazon; 1901 to Booth; 1922 broken up.
Obidense 1891-1901	2,380	1891 built by T. Royden and Sons, Liverpool, for Singlehurst; 1901 to Booth; 1910 to C. Olander, Frederikshavn; 1914 to Cuneo Steamship Company (S. L. Christie), Bergen; 1.1.1915 wrecked on the Shipwash Sands, on passage Rotterdam to New York.
Grangense (2) 1892-1901	2,162	1892 built by Palmer and Company, Newcastle, as *Ruggiero Settimo* for Italo-Britannica Royal Italian Mail Steam Navigation Company (A. Serena), London; 1892 to Singlehurst, renamed *Grangense*; 1901 to Booth; 1910 to M. Gumuchdjian, Constantinople, renamed *On Temmouz*; 7.3.1915 sunk by Russian Navy in the Black Sea, near Eregli.
Cametense 1894-1901	2,184	1891 built by Palmer and Company, Newcastle, as *Carlo Poerio* for Italo-Britannica Royal Italian Mail Steam Navigation Co. (A. Serena), London; 1894 to Singlehurst, renamed *Cametense*; 1901 to Booth; 1909 to Eastern Shipping Company, Penang, renamed *Tong Hong*; 1914 to G. McBain, Singapore; 1916 to Tan Kah Tee, Singapore; 27.7.1917 torpedoed and sunk in the Mediterranean, S.W. of Cape Sicie.
Fluminense 1894-1901	2,154	1891 built by Palmer and Company, Newcastle, as *Il Principe Di Napoli* for Italo-Britannica Royal Italian Mail Steam Navigation Co. (A. Serene), London; 1894 to Singlehurst, renamed *Fluminense*; 1901 to Booth; 1909 to E. A. de C. Martins, Para, renamed *Amazonia*; 1915 to Lawrence Smith Inc., New York; 1920 to Schemeil and Dilavery,

73

Name and Period in Fleet	Gross Tons	History
		Alexandria; 1923 to Egyptian Maritime Enterprise Company, Alexandria; 1927 to A. Khouri Haddad, Alexandria; 1928 broken up in Italy.
Santarense 1895-1896	2,898	1891 built by Nederlandsche S.M., Rotterdam, as *Didam* for Holland Amerika Line (N.A.S.M.), Rotterdam; 1895 to Singlehurst, renamed *Santarense*; 18.6.1896 lost in the Atlantic in position 15N, 33W, following collision with the barque *Dundonald*, on passage Liverpool to Para.
Madeirense 1895-1901	2,831	1891 built by Bonn and Mees, Rotterdam, as *Dubbeldam* for Holland Amerika Line (N.A.S.M.), Rotterdam; 1895 to Singlehurst, renamed *Madeirense*; 1901 to Booth; 1910 to Norwegian owners; 30.7.1912 stranded on Bird Rock, Bahamas, on passage New York to Port Antonio, declared a constructive total loss.
Mara 1898-1901	1,448	1883 built by Palmer and Company, Jarrow, as *Lady St. Germans* for St. Germans Steamship Co. Ltd., Newport; 1887 to Oriental Steamship Co. Ltd., London; 1892 to Demerera and Berbice Steamship Co. Ltd., London; 1893 renamed *Mara*; c1898 to F. S. Holland, London; 1898 to Singlehurst; 1901 to Empreza Nav. Gram Para (F. Gomes and Company), Para, renamed *Amazonas*; 1907 to Lloyd Brasiliero; 1930 broken up.
Napo 1898-1901	1,091	1897 built by S. P. Austin, Sunderland, as *Harmony* for J. & C. Harrison, London; 1898 to Singlehurst Iquitos, renamed *Napo*; 1901 to Iquitos; 1911 to Booth; 1913 to Reval Shipping Company (Joh Pitka and Company), Reval, renamed *Kodumaa*; 1919 transferred to Estonian flag; 1930 to Tallinn Shipping Co. Ltd., Tallinn; 1941 to Ministry of War Transport; 26.9.1942 wrecked off Goole after being damaged by air attack.
Ucayali 1898-1901	1,052	1898 built by Wood, Skinner and Company, Newcastle, as *Paris* for F. C. Strick and Company; 1898 to Singlehurst Iquitos, renamed *Ucayali*; 1901 to Iquitos; 1911 to Booth; 1914 to Leopold Walford and Company, renamed *Stanislas*; 1915 to Geo. Gibson and Company, Leith; 1932 to Greek owners; 1933 to G. Riccardi, Naples, renamed *Pescara*; 1937 to Soc. Anon Navigazione e

Name and Period in Fleet	Gross Tons	History
		Transporti "Sanet", Rome; 1950s to Soc per Azioni Navagazione e Transporti, Venice; 1960 broken up in Italy.
Javary 1899-1901	1,249	1898 built by S.P. Austin, Sunderland, as *Harlech* for J. & C. Harrison, London; 1899 to Singlehurst Iquitos, renamed *Javary*; 1901 to Iquitos; 1911 to Booth; 1914 to Garland Steamship Corp., New York; 1921 to Javary Steamship Corp., U.S.A.; 1922 to Donald Bros., U.S.A., renamed *Jeanette*; 1926 to G. Warner, U.S.A., renamed *Donnette*; 1927 lost—no other details.
Maranhense (3) 1899-1901	2,767	1890 built by Caird and Company, Greenock, as *Gulf of Lions* for Gulf Line; 1899 to Singlehurst, renamed *Maranhense*; 1901 to Booth; 1910 broken up by J. J. King and Company, Garston.
Amazonense (3) 1899-1901	2,828	1899 built by D. J. Dunlop and Company, Glasgow, for Singlehurst; 1901 to Booth; 1911 to W. Holzapfel; 1912 to Akties Damps. Sigrun (H. M. Wrangell), Haugesund, renamed *Sigrun*; 11.6.1917 torpedoed and sunk S.W. of Ireland.
Cearense (3) 1900-1901	2,769	1891 built by Naval Construction and Armament Company, Barrow as *West Indian* for West India and Pacific Steamship Co. Ltd.; 1900 to Frederick Leyland and Co. (1900) Ltd.; 1900 to Singlehurst, renamed *Cearense*; 1901 to Booth; 1911 to W. H. A. Walker (Coast Steamship Company), Liverpool; 1912 same owners, managers changed to C. L. Dimon, New York; 1913 to J. F. O'Meara (C. L. Dimon), New York, but still flying the British flag; 13.9.1913 wrecked at the mouth of the Nelson River, on passage Hudson's Bay to Halifax.

14. APPENDIX THREE
VESSELS OPERATED IN NORTH BRAZIL AND THE RIVER AMAZON

Reproduced hereunder is a fleet list of craft employed in North Brazil and the River Amazon by Booth (Brasil) Ltd., formerly Booth and Co. (London) Ltd., and Booth and Company. These interests and surviving vessels were disposed of prior to 1972. This list is not complete and full details are not available.

RIVER STEAMERS

Name	Gross Tons	History
Arctic	333	1906 built; Port of registry—Iquitos.
Baltic	332	1906 built; Port of registry—Para.
Acre	220	1911 built by Lytham Shipbuilding and Engineering Co. Ltd., Lytham; Port of registry—Para.
Beni	469	1911 built by Lytham Shipbuilding and Engineering Co. Ltd., Lytham; Port of registry—Para.

TUGS

Name	Gross Tons	History
Aguia	-	1900 built by Cochrane, Annan.
Anta	43	1887 built by W. H. Potter and Son, Liverpool, for R. Singlehurst and Company, Para; 1901 to Booth.
Rebocador	-	1867 built by Woodhouse, South Shields. (Wooden hull).
Criado	-	No details.
Papagaio	-	No details.
Aranha	-	No details.
Lontra	-	No details.
Conqueror	112	1897 built by Cox and Company, Falmouth, for Swansea Steam Tug Owners (J. M. Thomas), Swansea; 1900 to Booth, Port of registry—Para; late 1960s sold.
Parnahybano	-	No details.

Name	Gross Tons	History
Argus	-	No details.
Hercules	-	No details.
Sao Bento	-	11.4.1907 bought by Booth from Hamburg Sud Amerikansche Dampfshiffants Gesellschaft, Hamburg, (Hamburg Sud Amerika Line), through H. E. Moss, Liverpool; 30.6.1907 lost in Bay of Biscay while in tow of steamer *Cordoba* destined for River Amazon.
Manati	58	1907 built by P. McGregor, Kirkintilloch; Port of registry—Iquitos.
Mero	58	1909 built by Scott and Sons, Bowling (Yard No. 211); Port of registry—Maranham.
Guarany	26	1910 built by A. Rutherford and Company, Birkenhead; Port of registry—Ceara; (Wooden hull).
Pelorus	128	1911 built by Scott and Sons, Bowling (Yard No. 229); Port of registry—Manaos; late 1960s sold.
Wanda	-	No details.
Sarah	-	No details.
Arary	88	1913 built by Philip and Son Ltd., Dartmouth, for Amazon River Steam Navigation Co. (1911) Ltd., Para; 1915 to Booth, Port of registry—Manaos.
Ben	18	1920 built.
Timoteo	-	No details.
Florancia	-	No details.
Anacuan	-	No details.
Jurema	-	No details.
Bolivar	17	1952 built.
Stemwinder	118	1941 built; acquired post-war; c1970 sold.
Zulia	150	1944 built; acquired post-war; mid-1950s sold to Wilson, Sons S/A, Rio de Janeiro.

LIGHTERS

Name	Year Built (if known)	Deadweight Capacity	Name	Year Built (if known)	Deadweight Capacity
Sao Luis	1902	180	Elba	1948	60
Sant Anna	1902	180	Maioba	1909	65
Alcantara	1913	85	Moropoia	1910	65
Ambude	1913	85	Eva	1948	60
Arraial	1913	80	Lapa	1909	60
Tainha	1951	85	Maguary	1902	150
Traira	1951	85	Santa Helena	1901	700
Parnaiba	1882	90	Santa Monica	1901	800
Marreca	1911	80	Santa Barbara	1901	800
Minerva	1910	80	Armador	-	100
Marium	1910	80	Mercador	-	120
Mutuca	1910	80	Trafego	-	120
Bomfim	1910	60	13	-	150
Jordoa	1910	60	15	-	140
Furo	1909	60	17	-	140
Pindoba	1910	60	Tamuaia	-	150
Elvira	1935	60	Timbira	-	150
Esperanca	1922	60	20	-	200
Cambio	-	200	Caba	-	200
Secunda	-	200	Tertia	-	200
H	-	400	Pacific	-	400
BBL 6	-	190	BBL 16	-	190
BBL 26	-	190	BBL 7	-	190
Esther	-	70	Emily	-	70
Artic	-	600	Cedric	-	500
21	-	200	22	-	200
Elefanta	-	200	Urso	-	200
Tambaqui	-	150	Tucanare	-	150
Burity	-	200	Boa Vista	-	200
Brejo	-	200	Cecilia	-	30
Carmelia	-	30	Carolina	-	30
Candida	-	30	Claudia	-	30
Carlota	-	30	Clara	-	30
Catharina	-	30	Camila	-	30
Edith	-	50	Elena	-	60
Elise	-	60	Enid	-	70
Para	-	14			

WATER BOATS

Name	Year Built	Deadweight Capacity
Cutim	1909	60
No. 1	1923	8

ROW BOATS

Name
Amazonas
Urano

15. APPENDIX FOUR
VESSELS OPERATED IN PORTUGAL

Reproduced hereunder is a fleet list of craft employed in Portugal by Empreza Transportes Fluviais e Maritimos (Garland, Laidley and Co. Ltd., managers). The Booth Steamship Co. Ltd. held a 50% interest in the management company from 1912 to 1931, but had ordered tugs prior to that time.

TUGS

Name	Gross Tons	History
Mars (1)	47	1906 built by P. McGregor, Kirkintilloch, for Booth, on behalf of Garland, Laidley and Co. Ltd., Oporto; Port of registry—Glasgow; 1909 lost at Oporto.
Mars (2)	105	1909 built by Scott and Sons, Bowling (Yard No. 214), for Booth, on behalf of A.A.N. Decarvalho, Oporto; 1912 transferred to Empreza Transportes Fluviais e Maritimos (Garland, Laidley and Co. Ltd.), Oporto.
Jupiter	123	1915 built by J. Constant Kievits and Co. Ltd., Dordrecht, for Booth, on behalf of Empreza Transportes Fluviais e Maritimos (Garland, Laidley and Co. Ltd.), Lisbon.

ABBREVIATIONS

BOOTH	1. Alfred Booth and Company (1865-1881).
	2. The Booth Steamship Co. Ltd. (1881-1901).
	3. The Booth Steamship Co. (1901) Ltd. (1901-1920s).
	4. The Booth Steamship Co. Ltd. (1920s to date).
Booth Iquitos	The Booth Iquitos Steamship Co. Ltd.
Singlehurst	R. Singlehurst and Company—The Red Cross Line.
Singlehurst Iquitos	The Red Cross Iquitos Steamship Co. Ltd.
Iquitos	The Iquitos Steamship Co. Ltd.
L + H	Lamport and Holt Line Ltd.
BSL	Blue Star Line Ltd.
Austasia	Austasia Line.

NOTES

NOTES